Sister Surrendered

DARLA M. GRESE

ISBN: 1497541204
ISBN-13: 978-1497541207

DEDICATION

For Kelli
Always and Forever, Your Twin
XOXOX
-Darla

.

CONTENTS

ACKNOWLEDGMENTS

This journey would never have been possible without support from my loving sister Kelli, immediate and extended family, acquaintances, and professional colleagues. Thank you Janine Latus for your inspiration. Stan and Shirley White for your abundant kindness. Chaplain Amy Johnson for your prayers. Julie Driscoll for your guidance. Hutson Talent, Maultsby Talent, and Actors Access for your continued confidence. Kim Forbes, you continue to change my life for the better every day. Paul Buckley, you are my hero.

So many friends stepped up, dropping me daily notes and well-wishes. Each of you has a special place in my heart. Carla Abrasheff, Shannon Baker, Sonja Chiappetti, Dee Clare, Kelly Costley, Holly Deal, Carla DeJesus, Douglas Flanagan, Sherri Garcia, Nikki Jones, Tammy Jones, Missy Laux, Cindy Long, Tammy Long, Dawn Markins, Kristie Morgan Meadows, Yvette Norman, Krista Parks, Jeannette Rainey, Tracey Rentas, Teddi Sipe, Cat Skinner, Stacy Terry, my entire Sentara family, and my cousin Victor Sorrentino. Thank you so much for caring.

And without my friend and editor Dr. Evan Fiedler, Sister Surrendered would not be what it is today. His polishing skills blew away every expectation I had out of the water. And I have no doubt that Kelli is up there rooting us on, waving her terrible black and gold Steelers towel.

Anticipating the launch of this memoir has generated even more continued support which has been truly humbling. Thank you Mike Beaty and Leslie Wolbey for the selfless offering of your photography, Night of the Iguana for your beautiful venue, and Ashley Fussell with Soirees by Lauren. You have all been amazing. Annette Stone your heart is pure, your spirit golden. Chef Luigi, your food is superb.

Brady, I'm sorry mommy's been on the computer so much these past few months, but I have great news, things are different now. Mommy's taking a break.

I love you.

THIS IS A TRUE STORY...

1
WHY

Growing up, I never envisioned a future without my sister next to me, I couldn't. Life without Kelli would never make sense. Why did it have to be this way? Why Kelli?

And now I'm left with emotions that I'm not sure what to do with, struggling with a naked aloneness. An identical twin is the security blanket we all long for, a lifelong being of lasting love and friendship. To have that abruptly taken away can rattle you to the core.

I am inviting you on a journey of disturbing twists and turns, riddled with circumstances that bind the soul. The events that take place are not for the fainthearted nor the weak. At the same time it's a memoir and a promise, a promise that I made to my identical twin sister Kelli embodied with laughter, heartache, transformation, and triumph. It is just missing the right ending.

2
ALWAYS AND FOREVER

I am surprised I even made it this far. My twin sister Kelli and I were born in February, two months before our due date. Kelli three minutes ahead of me and an inch longer. And she took great pride in always reminding me of that. Both of us being less than three pounds each, we were even given our last rites by the Catholic Priest from our church. It wasn't until after several long months in the hospital that we managed to make it home, Kelli a month beforehand, to the Jefferson suburbs of Pittsburgh, Pennsylvania.

Our house sat on a steep incline on Payne Hill Road. It was a monster of a hill, unfortunately once claiming the lives of both our pet dog Snoopy and an ornery duck named Huey. Yes, we had ducks. Cars flew down that road, and it wasn't uncommon amidst a snowfall to have a wayward driver grind to a halt in our front yard. It was really exciting peering through the living room window watching-hoping that something dramatic would happen. This was just one among many simple pastimes Kelli and I shared as children growing up.

We didn't have iPods, laptops, Kindles, or a Wii.

Like our neighbors, we had one television that showed soap operas and Steelers games. Which meant we either watched what was on or stayed busy doing something else. And we almost always chose something else. However, at night just before bedtime, we could choose one show of our own. For me and Kelli it was *The Dukes of Hazard.* Yep, we were those tomboys who shunned baby dolls and anything pink. During the day it was about getting down and dirty, riding big wheels, throwing footballs, and chopping down my mom's rose bushes with our new hatchets that our father bought us. Even Grandma Sorrentino once tried gifting her baby girls with dolls on Christmas Eve, which we hastily returned for a train set. A beautiful Lionel with a working steam engine, obnoxious bells, and screaming whistles. But at the heart of the set was a beautiful Christmas Village. Every year that Christmas Village grew, allowing our imaginations to grow right along with it. We could sit there for hours, one at the controls and the other managing the village.

Wintertime was never-ending in Pennsylvania which meant that a great deal of our time was spent tempting frostbite. Unlike kids today who might melt in the heat or suffer hypothermia in the cold, we didn't care. We stayed out as long as we could, only going in when our legs and toes were numb. Kelli and I were fearless daredevils searching for bumps and bruises. There was a metal handrail that flanked the sidewalk leading up to the house with only nine inches of space between it and the ground. We would trek to the top of our hilly front yard, lie flat on our backs in our red toboggans, and race towards the narrow open space under the handrail. Amazingly, we would clear that space without shearing the front of our faces off, but barely. We would notice our mom standing at the living room window yelling at us, but we never seemed to 'see' her.

We lived in a rural town surrounded by woods and trails which was paradise for spitfires like us. Along with our neighborhood friends, we would carry our toboggans to the woods looking like a convoy of snowsuits, moon boots, and bulky mittens. We tested the limits of our cheap red torpedoes, flying down hills like speeding bullets, somehow not killing ourselves in the process. One day though, my luck ran out. As I soared down the hill towards Kelli, who was already at the bottom, I hit one of our homemade jumps and rocketed into the air, high off the snow. I realized as I was airborne that I was in trouble, but in true daredevil fashion I didn't care. I eventually hit the snow and holy cow it hurt like a mother. My backside hit first and instead of providing me a cushion, it faltered big time. Pain! That's what I felt. It was pure and utter agony. My tailbone felt like it had split open and I started screaming. At first, Kelli and friends laughed hysterically but after my endless wailing they figured out that I was really hurt and not just being overly dramatic. I ended up in the emergency room getting X-rays. My tailbone wasn't broken, but it sure felt like it was; I couldn't sit comfortably for weeks. And as expected, Kelli howled, rallying all of our friends to do the same. I had to take a donut cushion to school. Not fashionable. Every ounce of coolness that I had achieved up to that point was gone, completely destroyed. I became the butt of all the jokes and usually with Kelli leading them. Kelli was a naturally funny person, and the more laughs that she would solicit the funnier she became. That injury, by the way, would prove to haunt me years later.

When Kelli and I weren't reckless outside, we wrestled on my parent's bed. Flip, twist, throw, and pin was the routine. We battled tirelessly. We did our best to emulate Hulk Hogan or the Rock n' Roll Express, pounding our chests and flexing our biceps. Our mom was constantly yelling at us to stop, tired of making her bed several times a day. We would tear that bed apart as quickly as she could fix it. She would scream and we would giggle, and then of course continue our good-natured beating on each other.

There was this one incident though when I did push the boundaries and fractured Kelli's arm. Kelli was downstairs in the game room doing a back bend and of course I seized the opportunity. I snuck up quietly and pushed her arm from underneath her. That didn't go exactly as planned though, and instead of just scaring her, I hurt her, a lot. Kelli ended up in a sling and I ended up grounded.

Our father returned home one day after work with a motorcycle for Kelli and me. And it wasn't just any bike, it was a lime green Kawasaki racing dirt bike. It was like two adventurers hitting the lottery. The only problem was, that we didn't even know how to turn it on, let alone ride it. I'll never forget revving that engine for the first time. It was really loud music to our ears. I fired it up first and shouted to Kelli, "Hop on!" Foolishly, she did. Without helmets or any shred of fear, we peeled off. I sported an accidental wheelie, but fortunately for Kelli her vice grip on the bike and me was strong enough to hang on. I opened the throttle as if I had been riding for years. But before I could react, we were headed straight towards our German Shepherd Charlie and I plowed right into him. Yep, I ran right into our dog. I knew how to start the bike but I hadn't put much thought into stopping it. Charlie was fine, but my mom, well, not so much. The following week my father came home with a red Honda 50 and the Kawasaki was gone. Nope. Never saw it again. I'm pretty sure weeks went by before my mom actually spoke to my father after that one. That didn't stop us though. We broke the Honda in beautifully, tackling jumps like Evel Knievel. We were insanely brave and when reminiscing, I literally shake my head at how we managed to avoid broken bones and repeat hospitalizations.

When we weren't tempting fate, we were searching for stray animals. We were animal lovers, something that stayed with us into adulthood. We had dogs, ducks, guinea pigs, cockatiels, hamsters, cats, and a pet turkey named Sandy. If it wasn't slimy and slithery, we were bringing it home.

When our dad brought Sandy the turkey home, we actually thought she was our pet, and we were convinced that we were keeping her. I mean, that's what he told us. So, why wouldn't we believe it? We refused to let our dad keep her outside because it was too cold. So being a good sport, he allowed us to keep her in the garage. Every morning before school we would visit with her, feeding and loving on her. We were the coolest kids on the street. After all, not too many kids had pet turkeys. She lived with us for weeks and truly felt like part of the family. But one day, when we got home from school, we discovered that she was gone. Our dad told us that she ran away and I'm embarrassed to admit this, we believed him. We grieved Sandy for several days, devastated at the thought of Sandy wandering around outside, feeling lost and alone. We even skipped a few days of school hoping to find her.

Thanksgiving Day arrived and there was nothing unusual, just a typical turkey and stuffing dinner. But after dinner, my father confessed that we had in fact just eaten Sandy! Oh man, were we angry. We had just consumed our pet turkey. The turkey that we had grown to love. It took us a long time to get over that grudge against our dad. I have to admit though, Sandy was tasty. My mom was furious that our father disclosed Sandy's death. We weren't supposed to find out the truth. Thanksgiving was never the same.

And then there was the hunting dog. My father was an avid hunter. One day he came home with a puppy Beagle which he proudly ordained his helper and hunting buddy. Kelli and I had other ideas. He gave the dog some masculine name that I honestly can't even recall, and then insisted that he stay outside in a pen. My father manly shared, "Hunting dogs are supposed to remain outdoors." But Kelli and I couldn't allow that. We would cleverly wait for our parents to fall asleep, and then sneak the sweet little pup into our bedroom. We named him Baby. Needless to say, that dog didn't hunt. For the longest time, our father never caught on. But one night, we got sloppy which caused us to get caught. I'm pretty certain that my mom actually knew what we were doing. But if she did, she never let on.

More animal tales. We had a big Italian family with

many relatives living close by. Our Grandma Goose (who inherited the nickname Goose because we couldn't pronounce her last name–and I can still hardly pronounce it today), lived on a farm with cows, ducks, geese, and other animals. She was a tiny, adorable, deaf-as-a-door-knob sweet woman. We learned early on that we had to scream in order for her to hear us, although she was amazing at reading lips. But even Grandma Goose fell victim to our love of animals. After spending the day together, one of many in the past, she was driving us home when Kelli and I spotted a 'free puppies' sign at a random gas station in the middle of nowhere. We begged for her to stop and just as she always did, she obliged. We strolled into the worn down gas station and spotted the pups. They were your typical mutts. Nothing fancy about them at all. But Kelli and I didn't need fancy, we just wanted one. So again, we began begging her. She told us to call our parents, "Get their permission first." Kelli and I instantly knew what the other was thinking. We will pretend to call because she can't hear! Yep, we totally faked the call, even moving our lips as if we were talking. Kelli and I were ALWAYS on the same page. That's the twin thing you hear about, something that's not explainable, it just is. After assuring Grandma that our parents said yes to the idea, we picked out our pup and headed home. During the entire drive home, Kelli and I were chuckling uncontrollably. We knew that our parents wouldn't say no to Grandma Goose. After the car pulled into the driveway, we sprinted into the house with the pup. And then waited. Once our parents digested the news that we had brought a dog home, they started asking questions. Kelli and I cheerfully began telling the story while Grandma Goose stood by us, proudly watching and smiling. And we were right. Out of fear of hurting dear old Grandma's feelings, we could keep the dog. We named her KD; the initials of our names. That gas station dog ended up being one of the best dogs ever. She was loving, smart, and loyal; especially to my mom who ended up, as usual, being the one who cared for her.

Next came Huey and Duie, our ducks. Now, I should note here that we didn't live on a farm, not even close. But at times it felt like we did. Our grandfather caved on this one. He took us to a friend's farm where baby ducks were scurrying everywhere. They were adorable, chirping and playing as babies do. Our grandfather's friend said that Kelli and I were more than welcome to have a couple if we could in fact catch them. So, being the competitive and determined young girls that we were, we started running, and running, and running some more. Our grandfather and his buddy were rolling back and laughing, clearly having no belief that we would catch a duck. But to their utter surprise & subtle admiration, we did! And we didn't catch just one duckling, we captured two!! So this time we returned home with two adorable ducklings without a clue as to where they'd stay. We had an above-ground swimming pool that had a large deck wrapping around it. My father fenced the deck in with some chicken wire and that became our duck sanctuary. My mom, just as she always did, ended up being the care-taker. She fed and watered them without missing a beat, just as she did with our pet rabbits, Jordache and Blackie. Everything was pretty smooth with the ducks, until one day, while my mom was crawling through the duck enclosure, Kelli and I seized a mischievous opportunity. Gleefully disregarding good judgment, we locked her in and ran. And as my mom screamed at us, the ducks began flapping their wings and flying around my mom's head uncontrollably. She was livid, rightfully so. Amazingly, we were allowed to keep our ducks anyway. But then tragedy struck. As our school bus was nearing a stop, we noticed a dead animal lying in the street that looked like a duck. And, it was. Huey was dead. The official cause of death...'ducking too late.' Our father buried Huey in the back yard. We then took Duie down to a nearby river, and released him.

Dad loved that river. Although he rarely caught any fish, he had an amazing amount of patience trying to teach us to fish. Let's face it, twin girls running around laughing, breaking branches, and skipping rocks wasn't exactly ideal fishing etiquette. But he took us regardless. And in the thick of it, Kelli and I learned to love fishing just as much as he did, if not more. Except this one time. Getting ready to go to the river, Kelli and I were loading up the back of my father's truck with the fishing gear. I was in the back and Kelli was handing me the gear. As Kelli passed up one of the rods, I yanked up on it, catching the biggest fish ever. Kelli! Yep. I sure did. I hooked her lip like I was setting a large mouth bass. Kelli screamed and I ran. And our mom, yet again, was heading to the emergency room. This time with a 'hooked' Kelli. They had to cut out the hook, and needless to say, we never made it to the river that day.

I could write an entire book titled *Twincidents* when it came to Kelli and me. There was the "railroad tie to the head" incident, the "tree-stand" incident, the "woods catching on fire" incident, the "house-party bust" incident, the "quit making out with my boyfriend" incident, the "blue satin pajamas in the snow" incident, the "dad's going to kill us garage sale" incident, and a laundry load of others. Regardless of the mischief we would get into, it was pure innocence. By no means were we perfect, making our share of mistakes like every other youngster turn adolescent turn teenager does, but our fun was truly without malice. In the thick of it all, our younger brother Andy was a real trooper. He distracted mom and dad just enough for me and Kelli to get into more antics.

Just as most twins, our lives were intertwined in every aspect. Besides sharing the same birthday, we had the same friends, we enjoyed the same activities, we shared the same room, and we took the same classes. We both played on the same competitive softball team, Kelli third base and me second. There was never Kelli or Darla, it was always Kelli AND Darla. That's just how it was.

Our lives were enmeshed into one, something that never changed, that would last forever. That's what we knew, and it's how we preferred it to be. Sure we fought like any other siblings, at times wanting to beat the pulp out of each other. But at the end of each and every day, we laid in bed, one of us in the daybed and the other in the trundle next to it, and we talked, and talked, and talked some more. We ended each day talking to each other just as we continued to do for the rest of our lives until Kelli's life ended. I miss those conversations, I miss the sound of her voice.

3
NAVY RECRUITS

Like any other ordinary day during our high school senior year we had a career workshop consisting of local colleges, businesses, and several branches of the military. In a strange twist of the usual conversation, after visiting the Navy's booth, Kelli convinced me that we were going to become sailors. Okay, yes, we cursed like them, but that's about all we and the Navy had in common.

The following week we ended up at the recruiter's office signing away our free-to-do-whatever-we-wanted lives. Kelli was ecstatic but I was regretful, convinced that we had made the biggest mistake of our lives. Perhaps a borderline insanity level mistake. After all, why would any teenager choose boot camp over frat parties and tanning beds?

After graduating from Thomas Jefferson High School in 1991, we spent the summer lounging at the wave pool, sleeping in late, and attending nighttime parties at the houses of whichever friend's parents were gone for the weekend. But September 3rd was soon approaching, speeding towards us like a rocket.

Just before we left, my family rented out an enormous hall and threw us a going away soiree complete with a disc jockey, open bar for the adults, and at least one hundred guests. The decorations were red, white, and green as a tribute to our Italian heritage. We threw our arms to the song "YMCA," muddled through the chicken dance, and grooved to "Push It." We danced tirelessly, cried secretly, and laughed hysterically. It was a perfect night.

Apparently all good things must come to an end though, including our freedom. One morning, one very early morning, our doorbell rang, and at that moment, life as we knew it was over. Looming between us and the great outdoors where we used to go with the wind, was the Navy Chief himself. The one who assisted us in pledging our lives to the military, skillfully guiding the tips of our pens with initials and signatures on dozens of papers.

My father welcomed the Navy Chief in as we appeared at the top of the steps, sporting our short new haircuts, resembling boys. Kelli and I hardly spoke. If we had, our cracking voices would have been exposed. My mom couldn't speak either.

We hugged our parents that day, something we rarely ever did. Although our family deeply loved each other, physical affection was not often shown. Our love for each other was simply assumed. An unspoken faithful understanding. But this day was different. Our mom was an emotional wreck and our dad had heavy tears in his eyes. We had never witnessed that before. Where we came from men didn't cry. They were tough, brawny hunters with workingman weathered hands with wrinkles and callouses that could tell incredible stories.

We left the house without looking back, got into the white town car, and pulled away. I chose to curl up in the back so the Chief couldn't see my devastated and distraught face. It took every ounce of energy I could muster to keep from hyperventilating, and at the time it seemed like the longest ride I'd ever endure.

We ended up at MEPS (the military processing

station), in downtown Pittsburgh. We sat in a room clustered with other scared teenagers sharing boyish haircuts and nervous faces. It felt like we sat there for hours although I'm sure that it wasn't. The entire time I knew that I had made the wrong decision and agonized over how I could tell Kelli. And then I realized I couldn't. It was done. It was K and D always. We made a commitment together. So we went through the motions of signing more paperwork, barely speaking along the way.

Finally, it came time to get sworn in. The final requirement before becoming official. And suddenly, I drew the line. I couldn't, and wouldn't do it. There was no way I was joining the Navy, Air Force, Army or any other military branch. I wanted to go to college and party like every other high school graduate.

When they realized that they couldn't convince me to change my mind, the Navy folks told Kelli to talk with me in private. She begged me to change my mind, "K and D always?" but I refused. Even though it broke my heart to even think about Kelli leaving me, I didn't care. *I didn't care? What was I thinking? Where is she now? Gone. And I care! Kelli, do you hear me?*

I still wasn't going. So, as Kelli swore in with the rest of the group, I called my mom begging for her to come get me. She refused. I'm sure it broke her heart as much to tell me, "No," as it broke mine to hear it. But she did prop me up with assurances that I would get through boot camp and ended with, "Stay strong." With my exit strategy derailed, I had no choice but to raise my right hand and swear in alone while Kelli and the rest of the group stood by and watched.

We were sworn in. We were now budding sailors and the next stop was the airport. As we marched up to our gate our entire family sat waiting, looking like they were attending a funeral. Everyone was putting on their brave faces, but it was obviously hard. After all, we were saying goodbye for twelve weeks which was a long time for our family to be apart. As the plane began boarding, we hugged and cried not wanting to let go. It was terrible, gut wrenching. I was really upset with my mom and felt betrayed that she hadn't been willing to rescue me from this mission, yet at the same time the realization that I wouldn't be able to see or talk to her was torment to my soul.

Once we were on the plane buckling ourselves in, I don't think Kelli and I said anything to each other. But then out of the blue, we heard our grandfather's voice. We looked at each other and simultaneously realized what was going on. "Holy crap, he's on the plane!" We immediately started slinking into our seats, mortified, when we heard him exclaim in our direction, "Hey Kel and Dar!" with a tone of a glowing smile. As the entire plane watched, Grandpa took our picture, waved, and then disappeared. So much for being cooler-than-life teenagers. We were totally humiliated. Today, I look back to that moment as a pleasant distraction from what we would face in the coming hours, days, and weeks.

4
EMPTY CUP

After a long day of layovers the last plane finally landed in Orlando, Florida. Unfortunately, we weren't there to visit Mickey Mouse, that's for sure. We were escorted to a white bus and piled in like cattle. Amongst a sea of panicked faces, Kelli and I went straight to the back, intending to hide as long as we could even if it were only for a few extra seconds.

You could hear a pin drop on that bus and sense tears of stress. I remember wanting to give Kelli a beating for what we were about to go through (and that was just the first of many beatings that I wanted to deliver). Knowing her as I did, I knew she was more nervous for me than she was for herself, so I could only get so mad. At the same time, I knew she was scared as well.

When the bus finally stopped, it was pitch black outside so seeing the natural environment was impossible. We sat there in nervous anticipation on that bus until the door suddenly burst open, and a very angry red-in-the-face gigantic woman stepped on. She immediately began shouting the rules, but again, all I could think about was wanting to beat Kelli.

We were escorted into a building organized as two lines along opposing concrete walls. Another woman then showed up with about the same attitude as the first. The two fiery-eyed women yelled what to expect, how to speak, how to walk, and how to breathe. It was made utterly clear that we were officially government property.

After this pleasant and thorough introduction, it was time for a drug screening before being permitted to hit our racks (which, in military lingo means go to sleep). Mind you, it was now about two in the morning and everyone was dead, exhausted. All we had to do was pee in a cup and then shower, which should have been no big deal. But it ended up being a very big deal for me, as I was suffering from terrible stage fright. After all, who can pee with a woman standing directly in front of you intimidatingly glaring as if you've committed some sort of crime? Right. Not many. And I was one of them. I couldn't go. Each time I tried, my bladder shut down, refusing to cooperate. I would hunker down as long as she would let me before being forced to go drink some more water and pace. I was floating. My entire company was nearly finished, showered, and in their racks while I continued to pace and chug. At one point, Kelli had snuck in a look but she wasn't allowed to talk to me. And by the judging of her expression, she had felt really bad, but evidently not so bad that she couldn't go to sleep. Lucky. Still not cooperating, my bladder eventually began to spasm causing agonizing pain. I was the only one left of my group. It was terrible. But finally, the woman caved and turned backwards on my last attempt. I would like to think that she felt bad for me but I'm sure she was simply hungry and tired of looking at my empty cup. I showered and then hit my rack, frustrated that it took a while just to find an empty one in the dark. Then, as I laid there, I noticed Kelli looking in my direction. We looked at each other, and at that moment, I knew she was nervous too. And somehow that made me feel a little less angry at her. That was the first time in our lives that we couldn't end the night in conversation, and it was hard. Really hard. *Kelli, if you can hear me now, I love you.* By the time I closed my eyes, I had nothing left, not even a tear.

5
BOOT CAMP

No more than a couple hours later, a screaming mad man appeared. He was extremely short with a goofy mustache and an obnoxiously loud mousy voice. I can still hear that tone today, and it makes me cringe. A female who towered over him in stature joined in the attack. They were our company commanders, our CCs. From then on, we referred to them as Ma'am or Sir. "On the line!" they synchronously shouted. Bewildered, we lined up with bed hair, bad breath, and all. We were then whisked off to the barracks, our new home for the next twelve weeks. The barracks was just like you'd see in the movies; A large, bare room filled with bunks. We were instructed to pick a rack and stash away our clothes quickly as possible into foot lockers. Of course I chose the bunk with Kelli. She took the bottom and I took the top. "On the line!" We hurried to our positions, standing erect with our hands perfectly positioned at our sides. Down the line they went, examining our footlockers, our stance, and toe alignment. Our anxiety increased with every bit of verbal battering. I was so distraught even my fingers were tingling. Some of the recruits' personal belongings were tossed into the middle of the room. Others were being screamed at and openly berated, which only added to my panic. One CC stood directly in front of me, nose to nose. He glanced at my name, my face, and then at Kelli's name, face, and then back to mine. Yep, he figured out that we were twin sisters. I was waiting for the same joyous excitement and fascination we have always known that usually came with this discovery. I was expecting the same inquisitive three questions that were always asked in the same sequence, "Are you related?" "Are you sisters?" And then excitedly finished off with, "Are you twins?" But I couldn't have been more off. Instead, he blurted to the company in a foreboding tone that there were a set of twins amongst them. Just what I didn't need, more focus on me, on us. He mockingly shouted that because Kelli and I looked so much alike, we would have to be separated to avoid any confusion. He then ripped all of my belongings out of my locker and insisted I move to the opposite end of the barracks. Yet another moment when I wanted to deliver Kelli an I-told-you-this-was-a-bad-idea beating.

Later that day after we were unpacked and settled in, Kelli came down to check on me. I informed her that I was leaving. I was going to tell our CC that I was suffering from some sort of mental illness and that I wasn't stable. Kelli didn't take it seriously until several minutes later when she saw me in their clear glass enclosed office. It was designed this way to enable them to have eyes on us at all times. Through the glass, I saw a horrified Kelli watching. I thought I did a pretty damn good job at pleading my case but they didn't buy it. They motioned for Kelli to come in, and I knew from the look on her face that Kelli just wanted to curse me out, right then and there, but couldn't. Which was more than satisfying to me. Kelli, as dutifully expected, confirmed that I wasn't crazy and requested to talk with me alone, which the Chiefs' reluctantly permitted. Kelli did her best to convince me that I could handle boot camp and that it would only get easier with time. I didn't believe a word she was saying. To me, it was a stubborn trap. I was stuck there. And for the record, it didn't get any easier. And anyone who claims that boot camp is fun is delusional. Just sayin'.

Writing this memoir is my conversation with Kelli. I have always been a highly private person, so sharing it with you, well, I'm rather uneasy at this point to say the least. Given that, showering was a trial. Being thrust into an open shower with other women was beyond humiliating. I was forced to abandon any semblance of my formerly modest demeanor. To make matters worse, the bathroom stalls had no doors. Open showers and door-less bathroom stalls which forced me to, well, eliminate certain activities in front of strangers. It was an awful scenario for my true reticent self. I spent the entire twelve weeks getting up in the middle of the night just to go to the bathroom. And even then, I often couldn't go, and remained constipated for days on end. Nights were hard. Although we had some down time before 'lights out' which is when most people wrote home, I'd usually sit on the floor between the bunks and pout. Kelli claimed that recruits would come down to her and whisper, "Hey Grese, your sister is crying again." Kelli on the other hand loved writing home, telling boot camp stories…

"Guess what? I've been promoted to section leader. I get to wear a medal on my collar."

"By the way, crabs, mono, strep throat, and yeast infections are going around our company. God I love this place!"

"Mom, Dad, Andy, KD, Baby, this is your Navy daughter. The recruit petty officer of course."

"I just got done making my section clean. I love having authority."

"I think we graduate on Nov 5. Tell everyone to come!"

Here are a few quotes from my joyful not-so-frequent letters…

"This totally sucks! I hate it here. It's hot; I'm tired, the food smells and the bathroom stinks. But other than that, I'm having a grand 'ole time."

"Tell him (our little brother Andy) never to consider the Navy because it's pure hell!"

"Our company commander is a psycho bitch from hell. She is constantly screaming. I'd like to kill her."

"It gets harder and harder every day! As far as Kelli goes, well, you know her, she will stand strong and tall until she can't anymore."

Okay, there you have it. I was a train wreck and it never got easier. And for the record, I didn't really want to kill the CC, maybe just hurt her a little. For some diminutive reason, I failed a lot of inspections. There was always an incorrectly folded towel, or my gig line was off, or the corner of my sheet was wrong. Always something, something small and meaningless. Meanwhile, at the other end of the barracks, Kelli was promoted to section leader which meant that she was in charge of the surrounding girls in her area. And that really ticked me off! I often wondered if Kelli would have been the scapegoat if she was noticed before me that first day. Guess we'll never know. Either way, it seemed like the more Kelli progressed, the worse I did.

After a few days passed, we were finally able to call home. We marched to a line of pay phones with the crystal clear understanding that we only had a limited amount of time to talk. But Kelli and I had a plan. One would call my mom while the other would call our Aunt Marie. Then, after a few minutes we'd switch. It seemed like a great scheme at the time, but in the end, not so much. Both our mom and Aunt Marie answered their phones, which was great. But when I heard my mom's voice, I began crying to the point where my mom couldn't comprehend anything that I was saying. I wasted every precious minute of my phone time sobbing. She finally asked to talk to Kelli because it was clear that I wasn't going to be able to pull myself together. Poor Kelli ended up spending the rest of her phone time consoling my mom because she was so worried about me. I'm not sure if those twelve weeks were worse for me or for my mom.

I suppose I could say things improved somewhat, because a few weeks down the road I managed to get promoted to a flag bearer, something I was good at. I loved marching and carrying one of the company's flags, and the fact that my friend Marion Jackson carried one as well made it even more exciting. Our company was K078 and our flag had an ambulance on it to represent the number of injuries sustained during the course of our stay. That flag was a vivid reminder of one of my biggest fears, getting hurt and being setback which would have meant staying there longer and not graduating with Kelli. My flag bearing days, of course, weren't without incident. One day we took to the grinder to march, just as we always did, with me leading the company. It had rained all night and there were puddles everywhere. As we approached one, I made a flash decision to march around the puddle instead of going through it. Needless to say, my company commanders went crazy on me. They dropped the entire group into push-ups and since I had to continue holding the flag they made me do one-armed push-ups. For the record, I never again marched around a puddle.

The saying that shit-rolls-down-hill described my workweek perfectly. Since Kelli was a section leader and did really well over all, she ended up in a cushy job. Me, well, I ended up in the galley serving line. I wanted to sling those brick mashed potatoes straight into her face. The only problem was that the potatoes were too thick and sticky to catapult. The food was hellish, forcing me to live on peanut butter and jelly (which, by the way, does nothing for constipation).

The galley was located close to the pay-phones. I could see them from the outside of the building. One day during workweek, I made yet another reckless decision. Without permission, I was going to double-time (walk briskly) to the phones and call my mom. And that's exactly what I did. I took off determined to hear my mom's voice knowing that I was risking getting setback from graduation. I could have gotten into considerable trouble, but I just didn't care. When she answered, I began to ramble with a frightened tone, worried that I might get caught. Then she asked if Kelli was there with me and of course I said "No!" proceeding to confess what I was doing. She was stunned, and frankly so was I. She finally convinced me to hang up even though I knew she wanted to stay on the phone as much as I did. I hung up, double-timed it back and never got busted. I got lucky that day.

During 'family visit graduation ceremony' week, my father actually purchased a van hauling my grandparents, parents, and brother on a long trek from Pittsburgh, PA to Orlando, FL. Our Aunt Vickie was already in Florida and met everyone there. It was awesome inside and out, and I will never forget the moment when we marched to where the families were gathered. I don't think I've ever held my head as high as I did that night. "Halt!" couldn't come fast enough. Finally, we could hug our family.

Graduation day was profound. I carried the flag more proudly than I ever had before. I did it! I made it! I was a member of the United States Navy. *Thanks to you, Kelli.* And I was proud of it. I made some real friends during those twelve grueling weeks who have stayed close to my heart over the years. And any one of them can spin the yarn about trying times in boot camp.

6
GREAT LAKES "A" SCHOOL

After a couple of weeks of rest and relaxation at our parents house we were off to the Great Lakes for Hospital Corpsman School. Kelli and I carried a soft spot for the elderly. Our initial plan before Kelli discovered the Navy was to go to nursing school. We even toured a Catholic nursing school in Pittsburgh. I remember walking through the hallways passing several nuns. And somehow boot camp seemed like a better alternative? At least becoming a Hospital Corpsman provided us the ability to still dabble in patient care.

It was friggin' cold outside there and even being from Pittsburgh didn't prepare us for the Illinois cut-to-the-bone chilling temps. But I was elated. Boot camp was finally over and I felt human again. We checked into our barracks (BEQ) and discovered that we would be sharing the room with two other girls. That was completely fine with me, Kelli and I were still together and that's what mattered. We had enlisted on the buddy system which only guaranteed us boot camp and "A" School together. This was our "A" school. Beyond training, there were no guarantees.

A few good friends from boot camp were enrolled in

the same class; Allison Lutz, Joan Lidgett, and Chrissy Yurchak. And in some odd way cramming into a small room with three other people didn't seem so bad after all. Even the community showers and toilets had doors. It was smooth sailing.

Most of our days were spent in a classroom just like any other school. It felt very normal with the exception of marching to and from lunch and wearing uniforms. We had three different instructors and they were all easy going and relaxed, which was another breath of fresh air.

On the first day of class we were instructed to choose two color guard members to represent our class. They would lead our class during marches, attend practices each week with other teams, and perform flag-raising ceremonies during the morning colors. I shot my hand up, was selected, and even got to choose my partner. Of course I chose Kelli. Not only did we stand out, being twins made us jump out even more. Everywhere we went we were stopped. Everything about us was identical; our faces, our hair, our eyes, our ribbons, and our yellow ropes. I found it hilarious, but Kelli not so much. Kelli liked the twin thing flying under the radar, but me, well, I thoroughly enjoyed the attention we attracted.

After class we would head back to the BEQ for some down time, hanging out in the smoking room laughing obnoxiously at whoever stood out that day. We chain smoked while pressing creases in our uniforms. This was my taste of the conventional dorm life that I would never fully experience. We would occasionally study, but for the most part wrestled around in our racks.

The weekends were crazy. Every Friday night the Helm Club became the ritual. It was the nightclub on base for the enlisted. Our command consisted of several schools and programs in addition to Corps School, so the Helm Club is where everyone would come to mingle. I was introduced to line dancing and two-stepping. The ladies on base outnumbered the guys ten-fold so we were never without a dance partner. I was having a blast! We even decided to get tattoos. That's what sailors do, right? It felt like a rite of passage, a must-do. I decided on an anchor wrapped around a rose below my bikini line. Now, years later, it just looks like a smudge. But back then it looked dainty and I liked it, a lot. I can't remember which tattoo came first for Kelli. This would end up being the first of several trips over the years for us both.

Our Saturday nights usually consisted of renting a hotel room, getting intoxicated, and spending Sundays regretting Saturdays. To this very day the smell of Southern Comfort makes me nauseous. Kelli became good friends with a girl that was in the class just ahead of ours. She started spending less and less time partying with me and more hanging out with her new-found friend.

During our short tour there I even got engaged to a guy named Dennis. He got down on one knee on a Sunday morning and proposed when I was physically vulnerable and mentally absent. While a pounding head was squeezing my brain and dulling my decision making ability I squeezed out a response to his gentlemanly gesture, "Yes." But we never married. He was a great guy. Sweet, smart, and cute. And I'm sure he has made a great husband for whatever lucky lady married him.

On Christmas the school shut down temporarily so we were flying home. An alarming announcement came on while the plane was waiting to be taxied, informing us that there were difficulties with de-icing the wings. I immediately began to freak out. Kelli tried to convince me that we were safe but I was convinced that we were going to meet our maker. Kelli even approached a plane steward, spoke with him briefly, and then waved me over. He took us up to first class and asked what we wanted to drink. I chose a Long Island iced tea while Kelli had a beer. We sat on that plane for a very long time and I can tell you this, by the time we took off, I couldn't have cared less if one of the wings fell off.

While visiting our family in Pittsburgh I remember

counting down the days until we went back to school. It was nice seeing everyone but I actually missed my Navy family. Pittsburgh no longer felt like home for us. It would always have our hearts but it wasn't home anymore.

When returning to school, we chose orders to our first official duty station. The room was silent while our instructors prepped us on the process. Even if Kelli had chosen Alaska I would have chosen the same. *I would go anywhere with you Kelli.* My greatest fear was being separated from her. The thought of it sickened me. They presented us with a list of the available commands and the number of open billets (positions). The highest standing in the class academically to the lowest. Choices were given by that priority. Fortunately, Kelli and I did really well so we were near the top having more open options. The tingling fingers were back. I could hardly stand it. Kelli got to choose before me and the choices were vast. She knew that she faced persecution if she chose a command with minimal billets available. I would have bitten my lip, but been on fire on my insides. She chose the Naval Hospital in Portsmouth, Virginia because it had the most openings. Smart decision Kel! And then came my turn, and of course Portsmouth, Virginia it was. *Kel and Dar always, remember. Do you remember Kelli? Always. You are still with me. Here, now.*

Our parents drove in for graduation day. Kelli and I were leading the colors ceremony early that morning. We wore silver, shiny helmets, that again separated us from the group. The entire class stood at attention while Kelli and I led the ceremony. It consisted of sharp maneuvers, slow marching, and precise movements. Our parents proudly watched. It was an extremely emotional day though because we were saying goodbye to some of our closest friends with whom we grew to love. I had gained a whole new family and I truly loved them. We shared a lot of laughs, stresses, and growth that just seemed to mature naturally.

The military way of life is hyper-regimented turning you into a responsible adult without you even realizing its happening. This lifestyle has stayed with me to this very day. Sleeping past 5 a.m. is sleeping in, thirty minutes early is on time, and adhering to a daily schedule is the norm. Since finishing "A" school, every time I see the American Flag fully open and waving in the wind it still draws out a cornucopia of feel-good emotions.

My time in the Great Lakes made me realize it was the right decision, that Kelli had made the right decision for us on that once-upon-a-time high school day. I couldn't wait to begin our tour in Virginia. I was an adult now, not a scared young girl with tingling fingers.

7
PORTSMOUTH NAVAL HOSPITAL

Checking into our first official duty station was nerve wracking. I'm starting to now realize that most everything was nerve wracking for me. If you want to dissect and reveal all of your insecurities and imperfections, write a memoir. Anyway, when we first laid eyes on the hospital, we were blown away at how large it was, very intimidating, even a guard at the gate. After driving around the base thoroughly confused, we finally found check-in and the barracks. We had our own room. It was a breath of fresh air. Of course it was just another small room, plain and unexciting, but at least it was just Kelli and me. Our short term plan was to move off base anyway and get an apartment.

Our first job was answering command switchboard incoming calls. We actually got to work together! We once held a telemarketing job in High School that felt similar. We were terrible at it and honestly hated everything about it. It was excruciating for us not to laugh while reading our scripts. Now, graduates of Boot Camp and "A" school, we took this job very seriously. We answered phones every day, all day, and had a really good time doing it. It was a cake walk compared to everything else thus far. But we knew this was only temporary.

I became a beach bum almost immediately. I went to the beach as often as I could, every weekend unless I had duty. We were making a lot of friends quickly and everything seemed perfect. I did have one minor incident though, early on. Really, are you surprised? While we still worked at the switchboard I spent a Sunday at the beach, all day, without sun block. There were some beers involved as well. I had gotten so burnt that my eyes swelled shut. Yep, I woke up on Monday and couldn't even see myself in the mirror. In the Navy's eyes I had destroyed government property, literally. I was sent to the emergency room, put on meds, and then assigned to bed rest. I don't know that I ever felt pain like I did that day. My Leading Petty Officer (LPO) could have written me up and sent me to Captain's Mast, but he didn't. I could have been busted back in rank, lost money, put on restriction etc. I got lucky though, and Kelli, optimistic as usual, reminded me of that often.

Surprisingly, we were then both assigned together again, to the emergency room. We were astounded that they were keeping us together. We worked the day shift, finally getting to do what we went to school for. We did everything; including starting IVs, distributing medications, and drawing arterial blood gases. The same activities that nurses do in the civilian sector. And we were thrilled that we got to wear scrubs. No more uniforms. We started making an entirely different group of friends, including a guy named Tim who I met at a party and started dating. His quadriceps are what caught my attention leading up to his soulful blue eyes. I had never seen legs like that before, all cut muscle with discrete lines. He was training for BUDS (Basic Underwater Demolition/SEAL School).

During this ER rotation, sadly, Grandma Goose passed away which created a difficult situation since we both worked the day shift. After returning from the funeral, our LPO decided that Kelli and I needed to be on different shifts. This was the first time that we were separated on this rotation, but at the same time, we understood why it was necessary.

We rented an apartment with a close friend (Lidgett) in Churchland, VA, which was only ten minutes from the base. It was tiny but we weren't disappointed. Finally, we had our own bathroom and that was heaven! We bought a couch at the thrift store for ten bucks, had a plastic dining room table, and cheap décor. Kelli and I were never high maintenance or material girls so to splurge on fancy furniture didn't make sense.

However, splurging on a dog did make sense and that's exactly what we did. We went to the local pet shop at the mall and bought a Pekingese puppy. We named him Chewbacca. He was adorable with a smashed-in face and crooked teeth. Our good friend Matt would borrow Chewy to take him down to the beach to pick up girls. Chewy was just that cute.

Eventually, Kelli had a friend who ended up staying at our place rather frequently. She was stationed on the USS Puget Sound, a local Navy ship. She and Kelli remained really tight so most of Kelli's time was spent with her while mine with our roommate.

For the duration of my stay at Portsmouth I developed an amazing friendship with Matt. We were true buddies. I could tell him anything. We spent a lot of time partying, probably more than we should have; but hey I was only twenty years old at the time. Looking back, wow twenty, I had a lot of mature experiences, professional training, and subsequent serious responsibility at such a young age. Anyway, beer bongs and drinking games are what we really enjoyed, and truthfully, I was really good at both. Matt understood me and I understood him. We laughed constantly and maybe if things were different, perhaps if I were different, Matt and I would have ended up together in a much different capacity. We spent many mornings hooked up to IVs that conveniently hung from the ceiling fan, although I'm not sure how those were acquired. Kelli would come out of her bedroom, shake her head with disgust, and disappear back into her sleeping quarters. We would giggle as she did this. She was very much the mother hen, and me, well, I was the free spirit. She would have a beer or two and go to some of the parties, but she just didn't enjoy over indulging like I did. It was luckily convenient always having a reliable designated driver. *Kelli, you have always been my designated driver, in life. You still are.*

Kelli and I could visit home on this tour, quite a bit. It was about an eight hour drive from where we were but it was a pretty drive. It's oddly funny that Kelli and I would make the drive blaring Bon Jovi hardly talking to one another. It wasn't because we didn't want to. It was just that we simply enjoyed listening to the music and daydreaming. The few times we would talk is when it was arguing about whose turn it was to drive. Chewbacca was always with us, and at times we'd have a friend with us as well.

The time had come for blue-eyes to choose orders. He selected Gaeta, Italy and was due to leave soon after. When we left for the Navy, my proud Italian grandfather promised that if we ever got stationed in Italy, he would fly the entire family out to visit. Yes, I have a cousin named Vinny and a grandfather named Veto (and yes, that is the spelling we use in my family). Anyway, when I found out that Tim was leaving I was floored. That's when the Navy got real. This wasn't just one big party. It was the military and they will in fact move you. Naples, Italy was a large command and close to Gaeta. It was a more realistic option for me. Gaeta was small and there was almost no chance of me getting orders there, let alone me and Kelli. And there was no way I was going anywhere without her (if I could help it). So, being the rational problem solver that Kelli was, she suggested that blue-eyes and I get married which would in fact force the Navy to keep us together, or at least close. And just like that I was engaged, again. Tim was one of the most laid back, kind, authentic, and gentle guys ever. He always accepted us, Kel-Dar as a package deal.

8
I'M GETTING MARRIED

From the moment that I said, "Yes," Kelli immediately took on the role of wedding planner. Kelli and I went back and forth just as we always did on whom would tell mom. I wanted Kelli to tell her because I was too nervous. How would she respond? After all, it wasn't too long ago that I was engaged to a guy named Dennis. A guy my family never even met. This was a dynamic that Kelli and I had carried forward from a very young age. When we were children, during grounding or punishment, we would take turns writing my mom sorry notes. We would then go back and forth on who would run the notes out to mom. We would do this over and over again in an attempt to get our punishment revoked. Sometimes it worked, and, well, sometimes it didn't. Usually though, if we had something that we wanted to tell our mom, something that might upset her, we would usually tell our Aunt Marie first and ask her to tell mom for us. Ree, as we coined her, was like a second mom to us.

My family did meet Tim and fortunately liked him. So I ended up telling my mom that we were engaged. And although I don't remember the exact details of the conversation, I do remember the emotion, pure joy. Actually, everyone in the family was happy for me. If you haven't picked up on it, when you marry a girl from an Italian heritage you marry the whole family.

Kelli had less than two months to plan the wedding. Tim was leaving soon which meant that I had to think quickly. We had very little money so we had to do things frugally. I bought my wedding dress at a consignment shop. It was nice but nothing fancy. Kelli wanted to wear black, so black it was. Of course, she was the Maid of Honor. Ree's daughter (Chanele) was the flower girl, my brother Andy the ring bearer, and Kelli's on/off again boyfriend was the best man. Matt was the usher.

We decided on marrying at the chapel on Little Creek Amphibious Base. Tim loved the fact that I had Kelli because really all he needed to do was show up. *Yes Kelli, you have made it so much easier for so many to enjoy the grandest moments in life.*

Somehow Kelli managed to throw together an entire wedding and reception, invites and all, in under one month. Everything was black and white just as Kelli arranged; the napkins, attire, décor, everything.

As the wedding day approached I became more and more anxious. The fact was, I wasn't in love with Tim, the man that I was about to marry. I wanted to be but I wasn't. But I was doing what young girls do right? They find a man, marry him, and then have three, four, or more children depending on the extent of your big Italian family being involved. Right? Deep down, Kelli knew that I was struggling, but she never said so. She dutifully stuck to her role as the planner.

Our respective families booked hotels. The ring sizing was done. It was a definite go with everything in place. Before I knew it our families were in town checking into their rooms and settling in. Me? I began coming unglued. Not only did I feel trapped, but most importantly, I was hurting someone I cared about by not being honest. That's what was ripping me apart the most. We held our rehearsal dinner down at the oceanfront in Virginia Beach. The restaurant was a great steak joint, The Raven. On the outside, I was cool, calm, and collected, but on the inside a complete disaster. Yep, the tingling fingers were back. And to make matters even worse, I was meeting his mom and sister for the first time ever. I am actually getting married and meeting my future mother-in-law for the first time at the wedding. Hello commonsense, where have you been? *Kelli, you were an amazing organizer but shouldn't this have happened earlier? Oh, I see, that was on my list. I'm the one marrying the guy. Ughhh! Why do you have to be right all the time?*

Everyone except Matt and I were staying at the beach hotels. So Matt offered to drive me home. I barely spoke. He knew me well enough to know that something was wrong, really wrong. And he knew how to handle me, giving me space until I was ready to talk. I'm a mental food processor and he really knew it. He walked me in and then stayed at my place that night. No, I know where you are going with this. It was completely harmless. And Tim fully accepted my friendship with Matt and trusted him. I remember sinking into my waterbed and having a complete meltdown. I had held it in long enough and just couldn't any longer. I peered through my door into the living room to see if Matt was still awake. He was. And in true Matt fashion, he just listened through the darkness, never once telling me not to marry Tim.

Kelli, on the other hand, was having the time of her life down at the beach. Tim had a lot of Navy SEAL friends and apparently, late at night, some of them climbed up onto the hotel balconies into my mom's room and scared the heck out of her and Kelli. Hilarious! I was having a waterbed meltdown while Kelli was hanging with the Navy's elite. Perfect, not. Thinking back to Kelli telling stories from that night still brings a smile to my face. I mean, at the end of the day, Navy SEALS breaking into your hotel room in the middle of the night isn't so shabby right?

I woke up the morning of my wedding day with swollen eyes, open just enough to notice that it was freaking snowing outside. Either way though, I was getting married. Lidgett did my hair and then I was off, into the limo, heading to the chapel where I was going to marry a man that I wasn't in love with. A man that deserved so much more than he was getting from me. I felt really ashamed. He was a good man, nice-looking, smart, sexy, and kind. Why didn't I love him? I couldn't figure it out and it was frustrating.

When the limo arrived, guests were already being seated. For a 'thrown together' wedding, the chapel actually turned out very nice. We had a room full of friends and family patiently waiting. I found it hard to make eye contact with anyone out of pure fear that they would see right through me, and know what I was thinking. Kelli was so excited that day, smiling from ear to ear. And I knew that with her standing next to me I'd get through it. *Kelli you are really too damn good with commitment.*

When I was standing arm to arm with my father waiting for our queue, I realized that the back of my dress was stuck in the door. "Oh my God. Dad, I'm stuck!" He fumbled with the dress, freeing me to walk. As I approached the alter I felt like I was having an out of body experience. All eyes were on me, including Kelli's. Her smile lit up the room. And without a hitch, I was married.

Next came the fun part, the reception, which was also held on base. It too, turned out beautifully. But just as everything else in my life, there had to be some sort of "incident." As the DJ began announcing the wedding party, I began uncontrollably choking to the point where my eyes were heavily watering, with makeup running down my face. Just what a new bride wants, smudged makeup, smeared eyeliner, and everyone staring at you as if you were mocking the ceremonious rituals. Tim didn't know what to do, so he waved Ree down. She rushed to get me some water which eventually ceased the choking, but the embarrassment was incapacitating.

The reception continued on. It always continued on

with Kelli. The turnout was amazing, the food outstanding, and the music perfect. Kelli was too funny, making unplanned speeches about several of my once-upon-a-time antics, only the not-too-private ones of course. It was Kelli and she knows me. *You have always known me.* And to top the night off beautifully she caught the bouquet. Adding to the frolic, Tim's mom's boyfriend caught the garter. The celebration carried into a short honeymoon which entailed visiting my Aunt Vickie in Florida. Then, less than just one week after the wedding, my husband was off to Italy. Kelli and I ended up getting orders to Naples which was just about an hour or so away, so our plan had worked. Soon, it would be our turn to leave. Waiting to go, I backed off on the partying craziness. Somehow, I just felt different.

9
WEST VIRGINIA OFFICER

It was recommended not to take our cars to Italy for several reasons, including having to meet certain specs and theft. We made the decision to drive our cars up to our parent's house before our overseas tour. Days before we were due to fly out, Kelli and I made the trip home having a minor hiccup on the way there. Kelli's car followed mine as we drove through the mountains of West Virginia. I was driving a steady, speedy pace until all of a sudden a cop car appeared behind me; lights and sirens separated me from seeing Kelli's car. So of course I pulled over while he settled in behind. Kelli comically settled in behind him instead of continuing on which really ticked me off. I knew that she was watching and laughing hysterically while I tried to talk my way out of a ticket. He approached my car window and asked for the usual, "Driver's license, insurance card, and registration." He was actually quite pleasant though and became even nicer when he realized that I was active duty. He warned me to slow down but before he began walking away I asked him if he could do me a small favor. A little taken aback he asked, "What?" I explained that my twin sister was behind us and that she was driving just as fast as I was and I thought it might be funny for him to approach her and warn her as well. He surprisingly agreed to pull off the prank. As I watched through my rear view mirror, he marched sternly with a purposeful intent and form that said prosecute-to-the-fullest-extent-of-the-law towards Kelli's car. To this day, I laughed harder than I think I have ever laughed in my life. I couldn't stop. When she sullenly rambled through her glove box and handed the officer her info, I laughed myself to tears! This was the best practical joke ever. After just a few minutes, that seemed like an eternity for Kelli with her lip in a sunken pout, I saw her break into a smile. He apparently ended up telling her that since she and I looked so much alike, he wouldn't ticket us because it was too confusing. He was great. Officer West Virginia, if you are reading this now, Kelli and I say, "Thank you." I spent the next four hours alone in my car busting into spontaneous laughter.

10
BREAKING THE RULES

Saying goodbye to our family was different this time. We were going to another country for two years and although my grandfather claimed that everyone would visit, we knew that they wouldn't. This wasn't goodbye for a few months. This was two years for twenty year old girls. Back then, you didn't have email, Skype, cell phones, and iPods. Life was different and so was the sacrifice. Your daily communication just stopped.

This was the first time I noticed Kelli emotionally struggling just as much as I did. Anguish was written on both of our faces and somehow, in that moment, Italy didn't seem like such a great idea after all. But we were going, regardless, we signed orders. The morning of our outbound flight we were thoroughly exhausted carrying puffy eyes from a lack of sleep and tears. Saying goodbye was dispiriting. Still to this day, when I think back to that morning, I still get sad. That's how hard it was for me, for us. It's one of those moments that change and mold you into something different, a stronger person for getting through it. We weren't flying into a war zone, but that shouldn't minimize the pain that's caused by being torn from your family and closest friends. It was a significant amount of time in the mind of a young adult. Military members make incredibly huge sacrifices, and saying goodbye to the people that they love is just one example of many.

On the terribly long eight hour flight we were silent. Heartbreak had trumped my fear of flying. Not even turbulence stirred me up. I just didn't care. You see, I really did fall in love back home. But it wasn't with Tim. It was with a close female friend. And Kelli did as well, with another. Yep, there you have it. We were breaking the rules in the eyes of the military, and during those days, the majority of mainstream society. I remember in the early days of boot camp when we were called to the line and instructed to pull our watch-caps (winter wool hats) over our eyes so that we couldn't see. Our company commanders would then bluntly ask The Question, "Are any of you homosexual? And if so, please raise your hand." When we were allowed to lift our watch-caps, we saw that one girl was gone. Just like that. She was kicked out.

Kelli and I never had a specific conversation about our closest friends. Truthfully, we didn't have too, we just knew. We were those little girls who rode dirt-bikes, despised baby dolls, and chose camouflage each year for Halloween. Nonetheless, who we loved didn't define who we were nor does it now which is why I'm opting to skim over this pretty quickly out of fear that it becomes the crux of the story. Too often, someone's sexual preference overshadows their contributions to society, their academic achievements, their skills at a certain sport, their performance in a film or television show, etc. The reality was Kelli and I were wired exactly the same, and it was up to us to help each other work through it. We shared a mutual support system.

11
CAUGHT IN TRAFFIC

Once landing in Naples we were met by a couple of sailors who were assigned to us as sponsors. They took us to our barracks to get checked in, but Kelli and I couldn't ditch them fast enough. We just wanted to call home. We bought a couple of prepaid phone cards, found the pay-phone, and took turns calling. And as always, Kelli was able to keep herself composed, but me not so much. I was falling apart and Kelli did her best to keep me thinking positively. Kelli was my rock and she knew it. Which didn't allow her to crumble. *I'm sorry, Kelli, I'm sorry I was so selfish with my anxiety. Please hear me.*

The following day our sponsors' took us to our clinic where we would be working. It was about a 30 minute drive from our barracks and by the time we got there, I thought I was going to have a heart attack. We were warned that the driving over there was crazy. But holy crap it was insane! Stop signs, street lights, and the speed limit-all invisible. It was the craziest ride I'd ever experienced in my life. I remember me and Kelli sitting in the backseat glancing at each other, fear stricken, as we were being thrown from side to side. And the smell of Mt. Vesuvius filled the car as the smog thickened the air. Culture shock took over and we were already buried with uncertainty of what the next two years would be like. But we still had each other, we can do this, language barrier and all.

We arrived at the Pinetamare Branch Medical Clinic where we were both slotted to work. I cannot reiterate how great the Navy was at keeping us together even when they didn't have to. They could have sent one of us to the Naval Hospital and the other to the clinic, but they didn't, and we were seriously grateful.

We met our new Senior Chief. He was a tall, gray-haired, tattooed man. We just referred to him as Senior. He immediately took us under his wing. His most recent bride wasn't much older than we were and I think he felt the need to watch out for us. Senior told us about an apartment that was available three doors down from his house and we immediately moved in. We didn't have a car yet so he was kind enough to give us a ride to and from work.

In Naples, women were outnumbered by the men. The NATO and Marine bases were close by, both dominated by men. So needless to say, when word spread that there were two new females in the area, guys got excited. Especially when they found out that we were twins. It was kind of strange at times. It felt like men would jump through hoops for us and although we appreciated it greatly, it was still a little uncomfortable.

We were given a moped to use from one of Senior's friends until we got a car. Now we obviously knew how to ride a bike, but not in a country where people drove like maniacs. On our first night of having our new ride we were hungry for pizza. We knew of a pizza joint a mile or so away, so we decided to give the moped a try. We tugged back and forth on who was going to drive. Foolishly Kelli gave in and let me drive. And we were off! We sped out onto the gravel road that led us out of the neighborhood, momentarily fish-tailing but quickly regaining our footing. We eventually got to the top of a hill and came to a stop. We felt like the frog in the old video game "Frogger." That's exactly what it was like, one by one, speeding cars whizzing past us. I was so freaking nervous and I know in the back Kelli was freaking out, too. I suggested that we should get off and push the moped, but she insisted that we ride it, "C'mon' Dar, we're fine, just go." And so I did, aiming for a small gap that ran down the center of an over busy road. It was only a little wider than the front tire. And just as quickly as I approached it, I caught an edge and dropped the moped. And just like that we were lying down in the middle of bidirectional traffic. Oh man, Kelli was furious. Mostly because I had bent the tire making it no longer drivable, which also meant no pizza. I'm pretty certain there were a few choice curse words thrown around a bit as well, but we were sailors so cursing was the norm. Fortunately, down the road of life, we were able to laugh about that incident and did for many years past.

12
GOODBYE TIM

Telling Tim I wanted a divorce was agonizing, but after all, we were both in Italy now and I had to. I mean, that's why I was there to be near my husband right? He came to Naples, visited with Kelli for a while, and then we drove back to Gaeta, just the two of us. I don't know if I was more anxious about telling him that I wanted a divorce or leaving Kelli behind for twenty-four hours. But I had to. I don't remember the exact details of the conversation that we had. I think, in a nutshell, I explained to him that I realized after he had left that my feelings for him weren't what they should have been. And although he was hurt, he never got angry with me, something still to this day I'm so grateful for. He was a class act and a gentleman. There were a lot of tears on both ends and Tim will always have a special place in my heart just as he did in Kelli's as well. I gave him my beautiful diamond ring back, a diamond from his grandfather's cufflink, and filed for divorce. He and I never visited each other again.

13
ITALY

Our apartment was huge, as a matter of fact too big. It had two living rooms, three bedrooms, two bathrooms, and an enormous kitchen. That's just how the apartments over there were. And everything echoed because it was so big and empty with tiled floors and high ceilings. We didn't bother bringing our ten dollar hideous looking couch, so what little furniture we did bring, barely filled one room. At the same time, our new home was not so 'homey' at all. It was actually cold, quiet, and depressing. We had no phone, no computer, and no dog. We left Chewy in the states since we didn't know where we'd be living, but eventually he was flown out. In the meantime though, we got a puppy and named him Belinger. He was not so cute. His fur was a mixture of brown and black with a wiry texture. And his disposition was, well, unmanageable. We couldn't calm him down to save our life. He jumped constantly and barked continuously. Just terrible.

We eventually bought some living room furniture. We chose the small room in the back of the apartment to set up our cozy refuge. Kelli and I would spend most of our time in that room. We didn't have central heating, only kerosene heaters and bombala heaters which operated on propane. When you awoke in the morning it was freezing! I remember dreading the crawl out of my electric blanket, knowing that my feet were going to make contact with an ice cold tiled floor. One of us would have to go for it, rushing to get the heaters going in the morning. Winters were miserable and summers no better. We didn't have air conditioning so that left us sitting in front of fans hoping for some relief. It got hot there, really hot. And the plumbing system was hit or miss. Fortunately, our dad was a plumber so we were familiar with the toilet jack. We spent a lot of days snaking the toilets. If you got lucky the toilet would flush, but if you didn't, you'd end up with a sopping wet floor. We had to keep towels close by just for that very reason. They were our designated soak-up-the-overflow towels. Sounds like fun right?

Two girlfriends flew in to visit. They stayed for a couple of weeks and we had a blast. We traveled a little but mostly just hung out. For those two weeks I felt like me again. But then it was time to say goodbye all over again which threw me right back into my sad state. I told Kelli that I was going down to Senior's house to tell him that I suffered from some sort of mental illness, essentially making me incapable of staying overseas any longer. After the boot camp threat, Kelli knew I was serious. Behind flowing tears she begged me not to do it. We both were crying at this point. Inside, I knew that losing me to the states would devastate her and that's what ultimately stopped me from making that walk down the street. I saw a real fear in her eyes. I couldn't hurt Kelli by leaving. So instead I spent many days in my cold, empty room trying to release the sadness through crying. It took me a long time to work through those emotions. It was one of the most challenging times of my life and still brings up heavy feelings. Again, Kelli took on the pillar of strength role. Always attempting to talk me up when I was down. She let me have my moments of despondency and despair, never batting an eye, and then would jump in with a positive spin. I listened but found true solace and escape in beer. Every night beer was becoming my anecdote. That was the only way that I could slow my mind down enough to actually fall asleep. Now this really worried Kelli who rarely drank anything. She knew that I was homesick and slipping. I had spent the first several months in Italy with an obnoxious dog, bad plumbing, a home that breathed kerosene filled air, and little to no communication with our family. But Kelli worked us through it. I would have quit on this a long time ago. *Kelli, you had such commendable strength when it came to tough situations.*

14
CIAO KELLI

Through mutual friends, we were introduced to Shani working in the mail room at the Naval Hospital. We had a lot in common. A love for softball, close in age, and low key. Her laugh was infectious, such a welcoming sound. Eventually Shani moved in with us and she and Kelli grew extremely close. Soon we began making more friends and joined the hospital's softball team, The Scrubs. Coincidentally, Shani played shortstop, placing her directly in between Kelli and me. These are the days when my competitiveness in the sport skyrocketed. We had a great team, winning countless tournaments. Most of our weekends were spent at Carney Park where the games were held. Teams from bases all over would travel in to play us. One team was from the USS Simon Lake which was based in La Maddalena. I ended up making a lot of friends on that team, some to this day.

Kelli and I finally decided on getting a house phone which was a huge expense, but in the end, worth every cent. We could now call home. The calls were only for five minutes. Five minutes filled with tears of joy. The house phone returned the balance to my life that I was searching for. I even started playing practical jokes on Kelli again.

We did eventually get a car, a beater. It was loud and an eye sore for certain but at least it was transportation. There was a place down the street from where we lived that sold roadkill, which we in the U.S. call rotisserie chicken. Except their chicken was actually cooked outside over open flames and it wasn't uncommon that you'd find some charred feathers. But it tasted amazing. I have no idea where that nickname came from but either way, roadkill was to die for. Anyway, a man named Giuseppe (of course) ran the chicken stand. He was a local who hardly spoke any English. He had a huge crush on Kelli and boy did we give her a hard time. Every time he saw her his face lit up. I can still hear his voice, "Ciaoooo….K…ellllllliiiiiiiiii" Thanks to Kelli we got a lot of free roadkill.

One day Kelli and I were just hanging at the house, when all of a sudden the outside door buzzer rang. I remember us just slowly turning towards each other thinking, "Who would be visiting us?" It was Giuseppe. "If you open that freaking door, I'll kick your ass," Kelli whispered. So of course I buzzed him on in. "Ciaoooo….K…ellllllliiiiiiiiii," Giuseppe said over and over and over again. They spent the next hour or so smiling at each other at the kitchen table, until finally, he left. Okay, I deserved a good sisterly beating for that one. But thankfully, she just laughed it off with a healthy warning for me to never do it again. Giuseppe was harmless, a complete gentleman, who by the way never stopped by again.

When I think back to our Italy tour, a whirlwind of emotions take over. Those two years forced me into adulthood in so many ways. I cried a lot, laughed a lot, and learned a lot. And as soon as it began, that tour would come to an end. Sending us back to the states different people, appreciative of the simplicities of life, appreciative of each other, and appreciative of our careers in the Navy. We were both promoted to E-4 during our stay there, getting frocked at the very same time. We also re-enlisted for two more years, anxiously striving for E-5. And to think I would have quit.

15
ROBBERS, A GERMAN SHEPHERD, AND A BROOMSTICK

Only two weeks to go in Italy. The Navy had already 'packed us out' which meant that our furniture, belongings etc. were shipped back to the states. Kelli and I were house sitting for a nurse friend having already moved out of our apartment. She lived in a huge, three-story home and had a full grown German Shepherd that we were dog sitting, too. I can't remember his name but he had a contrasting sweet disposition to his very intimidating presence. Over the course of our stay at her place, we said our goodbyes, tied up loose ends, and prepped for the long trip home. We had both received orders back to Portsmouth Naval Hospital and were very excited. It was hard to believe that for another two years the Navy chose to not separate us.

On the night before our friend was due back home, our last night at her house, Kelli and I settled in. She and I slept on the third floor together. I recall that night vividly as if it were yesterday. We were excited to be leaving to see our family again, but we were sad to leave the people that we had grown to love in Italy. She and I laid in bed and talked for a long time reminiscing about what had passed, anticipating the near and distant future. Finally though, we ended up going to sleep. I slept closest to the door and she against the wall, closest to the balcony.

It was at approximately three in the morning that we were simultaneously awakened to a crashing sound next to me on the floor. It was the glass Gatorade bottle that I was drinking before we had gone to sleep. It was kicked over by a stranger. In unison, Kelli and I quickly looked to my right as a man intensely fumbled through the nightstand drawers, not realizing that we were watching. We were terrified. We didn't know what to do. We were both frozen with fear. As she and I slowly sat up, he saw us. Kelli began scooting herself to the wall behind her as I forced myself in the same direction, basically smothering Kelli until I couldn't go any further. The room was silent for a few moments, spooky silent. But then he began growling, sounding like a wild animal. In that flash by, we thought he was going to kill us, and truthfully, it would have been easy because she and I were fear stricken and defenseless. His growl became louder and louder, eventually graduating to a scream which we later realized was his way of letting his buddies downstairs know that we were awake. He then took off running downstairs as Kelli and I remained petrified and immobile. We physically could not move, staying coupled together in bed, frozen.

Minutes ticked by, or at least so it seemed, before we decided to look out over the balcony. We were hearing a lot of racket and commotion and couldn't resist. We watched three guys load up a car with our friend's belongings, and ours, and take off. They were laughing the whole time when doing it.

While thankful that they were gone, we still weren't convinced that someone else wasn't downstairs waiting for us. We wanted to get to the house phone but that was three floors down. So she and I began shoving each other into first position as we tiptoed down the steps, broom in hand. Yep, that was our weapon, a broom that I had just used the night before to tidy up. We were stuck together barely able to walk because we were so close.

At last, making it downstairs, we ran for the phone and then for the door. Our goal was to get out of that house as quickly as possible, all along confused and wondering, "Where was the dog?" Once making it to the street we called our clinic asking them to call security. And as we waited, we then called home. We first called our mom and then our Aunt Marie. After all we were just twenty-two, technically adults, but still emotionally very young. Crying and hysterical, we proceeded to tell them what had just happened. We were in shock and at the same time relieved that we weren't hurt, raped, or murdered. Over there, theft was unfortunately frequent with occasional violent crimes, but not as common. Not part of the occasional, we were the lucky ones. But either way it traumatized us greatly.

Security arrived with the local police and the entire house was searched before allowing us back in. The thieves had fed the dog a big piece of steak which he was still gnawing on. So much for an attack dog! It was discovered that our friend's house was cleaned out for the most part. Our gifts that we had purchased for our family were all taken. Even some of our clothes were taken out of the dryer. The criminals were obviously there for quite a while.

That same afternoon, we drove to the airport to pick up our friend and unfortunately had to share the bad news, "Most of what you owned is gone." Talk about a tough conversation. But she was great. The only thing that concerned her was our safety.

The Navy jumped on this right away, taking every precaution to make sure that we were emotionally okay. It was then that we were diagnosed with PTSD and rightfully so. Although unharmed, we were really shaken. Ironically, if that robbery would have occurred in the first week of our Italy tour, we could have transferred back to the states on hardship orders. But

I'm glad that didn't happen. I needed that tour.

16
COACHING AND OTHER STUFF

I have to say stepping back onto U.S. soil was grand. After two years overseas I returned home a more appreciative and grateful soul, as did Kelli. We as Americans are comfort spoiled with wall to wall carpeting, central heating and air, fast food joints, convenience stores, and so much more.

Checking into Portsmouth Naval was much different the second time around. We were returning as Petty Officers with a little time under our belts so the transition was nice. Instead of being shuffled into the barracks we were put up in the Omni Hotel in Norfolk. Our longtime friend Christy was still stationed there, so she gave a friend of hers' (Jaye) the heads up that we were coming in. Not only did Jaye keep us from the barracks but she also lined us up with nice jobs. I worked in the MMART (Military Mobilization and Readiness Team) Department and Kelli worked in the Command Fitness Department, which both happened to be in the same small building. We were officially paper pushers and weren't complaining one bit. We drove to and from work together, ate lunch together, and took breaks together. We quickly began making a lot of new friends and things were, well, for lack of a better word, perfect.

Within a month or so, we rented a small apartment in Churchland not far from where our first apartment was. This apartment, like the last one here, was tiny. Barely accommodating our sectional couch. As I said before, Kelli and I keep things as simple as possible. This time though it was a little different. It was quiet. My days of partying were done. I just had no desire. Unfortunately, we did have our share of nervous nights because of the robbery in Italy. That experience had changed us for sure. We were living pretty low key for the most part and it was nice. Christy and I remained friends until she moved back home to Georgia. Most of our weekends were spent fishing and watching football.

As our circle of friends grew, we eventually met a sailor named Susan who headed the Color Guard Team at the hospital. We quickly hit it off, sharing a lot of common interests. So Kelli and I joined the team. We were back to performing in flag ceremonies, retirement ceremonies, Memorial/Veterans Day ceremonies, etc. For a short while, we were an all-female team and were a prize catch sought out by surrounding commands. We earned an extremely respectable reputation, winning several awards and Letters of Accommodations. Kelli carried the flag and I maneuvered the rifle. In time, Susan relinquished the team to Kelli and me and we ran it together. The Veterans Day ceremonies were always our favorite. We'd have to report very early on our day off to a small cemetery located on the command. It was the kind of ceremony that would give you goose bumps.

We eventually ended up buying a house in Churchland with Susan. The house was perfect, sitting in a cul-de-sac with a generous front porch, decent backyard for Chewy, and plenty of inside space. The kitchen was huge which ended up being a popular gathering spot for whoever stopped by. I converted the room over the garage into a gym, and the garage, well, that ended up being the largest transformation of all. We had it insulated and dry walled, carpeted and painted. We even had the heat piped in. It became an amazing game room with a beautiful pool table, bar, and plenty of seating. That room saw a lot of house parties and pool tournaments, even one or two games of strip-pool, a subject that I will just leave alone, here, to your imagination.

We lived down the street from some softball fields that we would later find out were in need of some coaches. The three of us ended up taking a team of girls. They were middle school age and very competitive. We named our first team The Stealers, decked out in black and gold jerseys. Those girls clicked on the field in a fluidic sense and ended up becoming the team to beat. Those days were crazy busy for Kelli and me. In addition to working full time, we were running and rehearsing for color guard ceremonies, holding practices for and coaching The Stealers. But somehow we never missed a beat, enjoying every second of it. I remember coaching first base as Kelli coached third and realizing that we had evolved. We were coaches now and no longer just the second and third basemen. And we were damn good coaches winning season after season. What separated us from most of the other coaches is that we weren't out there 3 or 4 days a week because we had a daughter on the team, we were out there for the love of the game. When Kelli and I stepped onto that field our game faces were on and losing was not an option. And lucky for us, our girls were just as determined to win. We grew to love those girls and their parents as if they were family.

On the weekends that we were able to catch our breath, we would travel to a friend's house to fish. Thomas lived in Suffolk, VA, which was only ten minutes away. He had a beautiful waterfront home. And at that time had a pier that he would allow us to fish from. Half of his home was Nansemond River Bait and Tackle which he owned and operated while he lived upstairs. We would sit on that pier for hours at a time catching Croakers. Sometimes we would return home with a bucket of fish that we would have to filet, but that was okay, we enjoyed it. We loved our lipstick but could just as easily shift into ball caps, night crawlers, and worn jeans. On Sundays during football season, we gathered in the living room with a group of friends and watched the games (that we might have placed wagers on). Our roaring fire would get the living room nice and toasty as we cheered and cursed as sailors do at the television set. It was perfection.

17
SIX WEEKS

One Monday morning at work while I was doing the usual reading of command emails, an Urgent Request appeared. Squadron VF-41 needed a Hospital Corpsman to travel with them for six weeks. They were accompanying the USS John F. Kennedy based in Mayport, Florida for a short training stint. The ship was traveling to England and Ireland, which to me sounded like a free vacation. Now usually I would have taken the request to my Commander and not thought twice about it. But not this time. These orders were mine. So without mentioning it to anyone, I met with my Commander and begged her to let me go. Expecting her to say no, I was astounded when she said, "Yes." And just like that, in a couple of days I was leaving. Next came the hard part, telling Kelli.

When I shared the 'good news for me' that evening, her reaction was surprisingly out of character. As good as she was at pushing through conflict, handling challenging times and change, this one actually shook her up. It was the first time that we would really ever spend anything longer than a few days apart from each other, ever. This was the first time that I actually witnessed her fearful, instead of me. And in an interesting twist, seeing her upset forced me to take on the strong and courageous role. Even though the thought of leaving her was tormenting me on the inside too. Truth be told, after talking to Kelli that night, I regretted my quick, jump-the-gun decision. *I want you to know that Kelli. I regret it. I love you.* But by then it was just too late, my orders were already cut.

When Kelli dropped me off at the airport, we didn't speak, we just couldn't. I couldn't believe I was doing what I was doing. I felt like a scared little girl that was about to dive into unfamiliar waters without my life preserver. But that's exactly what I did. Kelli waited with me until it was time for my flight to board. And then. Just like that. I left. Never turning back. Fearful I would crumble.

I managed to stay composed on the outside, but on the inside my other half was no longer there and it was crushing. Yes, it was only for six weeks which I'm sure to most people sounds ridiculous. But when you're a twin with the kind of relationship that she and I had, it was different. Was it all that she and I knew? Yep. And I wouldn't have changed a thing about our relationship, not one.

Once arriving in Mayport, I made a quick call to Kelli knowing that I wouldn't talk to her again until we got to Dublin. Back then we had no capability of emailing from the ship to home, it just wasn't possible yet. Or maybe I should say, if it was possible, nobody told me about it. After being introduced to a couple more of the corpsman that were assigned to my squadron I felt a little more at ease. But then, what was supposed to be my liberating vacation quickly took another direction. I found out that this was a high profile visit to Dublin and that VIPs would be boarding once we got there. So that meant, cleaning, sleep a little, and then clean some more. It was terrible. I can honestly say that I've never, even until this day, ever worked that hard! Anyone that thinks that the ship life is easy, like I did, is sadly mistaken. There's no escaping work, it surrounds you. There's always some sort of bell or whistle, or an announcement about something. It's never quiet. And when it was time to hit our racks the jets were flying night ops. And I can assure you that F-14 Tomcat Fighter jets are not quiet.

But with the trials came amazing experiences. I got to observe the Changing of the Guard at Buckingham Palace. I learned how to properly pour Guinness in an Irish pub. And I learned how to drink Guinness properly in an Irish pub. I visited Big Ben in London and met a lot of very nice people. But after six long, exhausting weeks, I couldn't wait to get home. I had only talked with Kelli a couple of times so to say that I missed her would be an incredibly huge understatement.

My guys in the squadron took care of me from start to finish, taking on the big brother role. They called me Baby Doc. Even making me a badge for a souvenir. They also presented me with an enlarged photo of the ship and signed it with personal messages. They were a great group of guys and they made that trip as tolerable and as enjoyable as they could. VF-41 rocks!

When I first saw Kelli at the airport it was as if we hadn't seen each other for months. No, we didn't hug, we just didn't. But we talked endlessly late into the night. She missed me just as much as I missed her and those six weeks would end up being the longest that Kelli and I would ever go without seeing each other again. *See, I told you I made a mistake, do you believe me now? Do you Kelli?*

Shortly after my trip, Susan decided that she was going to move out which meant that Kelli and I would own the house together, just the two of us. It then came time for Kelli and me to consider two options, re-enlisting or getting out. We both agreed that we weren't going to sell the house and move again. We had only been back in the states for just under two years and we loved our old 'new to us' home. We attempted to get orders to a ship, but back then being female and a corpsman limited your options. There weren't any billets open for us. We also attempted to extend where we were. But that too, wasn't an option. So that left us with choosing to go overseas again, and that certainly wasn't going to happen. So we decided to leave the Navy after six years; six maturing, exciting, and amazing years.

18
ADDICTED

Although excited to begin our new chapters in life as civilians, we were also nervous and anxious. The job market was uncertain and we had a mortgage, car payments, utilities etc. There were no guarantees. Somehow though we were confident that things would pan out, perhaps a tad naïve. Kelli had dreams of becoming a boat captain for a local fishing company, and I, well, I wanted to become an actress. I ended up taking a job with Coca Cola as an account manager, even having my own company van. It paid well and also gave me the flexibility of taking acting classes at night. Kelli began working for our friend Thomas at his tackle shop. She worked the front counter and was having a blast. For a while our transition was rather smooth. A friend recommended we establish ourselves at the local Veterans Affairs Medical Center and to also file for disability compensation for diagnoses that occurred during our active duty service, such as the PTSD. So we did just that, filing the appropriate paperwork and establishing ourselves at the VA. We were assigned two different physicians, something at the time that seemed irrelevant, but later proved itself monumental. I noticed over time that Kelli was going to the VA rather frequently. More and more as time passed. And shortly thereafter, white plastic bags full of pill bottles were being sent to the house in startling quantities. Kelli was also changing, becoming more withdrawn, reticent, and appearing extremely depressed. And as more pills arrived, the worst things became. Even getting the attention of her friend and supervisor Thomas, who knew Kelli incredibly well. She was often calling in sick to work, sleeping excessively, becoming irritable, and spent little time grooming herself. She even started staying in rundown hotels. Sometimes for several nights in a row which was really distressing and scary. I tried to reach her but it would just turn into a rambling argument. Kelli even turned aggressive at times, going nose to nose with me, screaming like we were two strangers. I felt like I was living in a nightmare. I had never experienced anything like this with Kelli. Even her daily functions crumbled. I remember vividly at one point during breakfast when her face just dropped directly into her cereal bowl. After this had gone on for several months, I deliberately approached Kelli with a more stern demeanor.

She was sitting in the kitchen. Her spirit gone and her eyes empty. We both cried as I begged her to get help. She admitted that she was addicted to the pills that the VA was dispensing, specifically Klonopin and Ativan. Thinking back to that morning nearly sixteen years later, it still drives a sharp pain deep into my chest. A stifling heartache. That was just the beginning of a nightmare that I would never wish on anyone. My twin sister, my pillar of strength, my idol of certainty, my other half, was changed forever. *I know you were in there. Behind that curtain of intoxication. I know you Kelli.*

19
5000+

I convinced Kelli to check into the hospital to detox from the pills. I even drove her to the VA where she was admitted to the inpatient psychiatric unit. Saying goodbye to her as two heavy doors slammed in between us is a memory that would forever haunt me. A wall that should have never been. I sat in the parking lot of the hospital and sobbed, not being able to convince myself to drive away. This wasn't supposed to happen. It wasn't in the cards. I was the one who was supposed to fold under pressure and collapse, not Kelli. I wasn't strong enough for this, not this, not Kelli.

Once home, I immediately went into detective mode scouring through Kelli's bedroom. I found bottles of pills from the VA hidden everywhere. There were bottles in socks, clothes, pockets, a Kleenex box, and stuffed under her mattress. Kelli hid them in places that most would never think to look. But I was her twin and knew her best. I left nothing unturned, no corner and/or crevice unexamined. My goal was to ensure that when Kelli returned home, the house would be poison free. By the time I finished tearing up her room, I had a mountain of bottles. I was speechless. I couldn't believe what I was seeing. It was no wonder why Kelli couldn't hold her head up. My friend Maureen, there with me, was dumbfounded. While we sat there in awe of what we were seeing, the phone rang. I shot up quickly because I knew that it was Kelli. And I was right, it was her, crying and hardly able to speak. I cried as well while attempting to comfort her. Making certain that she knew that everything would be okay. She begged me to come the following day for visiting hours and of course I said yes. The thought of her sitting in that locked unit made me cringe. I hated it. Every f-ing second of it. I hardly slept that night. Constantly thinking and wondering about Kelli and how she was doing. I counted down the minutes until I could go to her, just sit with her. My Kelli. I couldn't help but think back to our childhood, boot camp, and every other aspect of our lives together, good, challenging, hard, rewarding, enduring. Enduring. *Kelli, damn it, you had it, you had the secret, you loved life and it loved you back, ughhhh*! I wondered how an individual like Kelli who was so strong, brave, determined, and solid could fall from grace so rapidly.

As I waited to get buzzed into the unit my heart was pounding out of my chest. I didn't know what to expect, what she would look like, or what she would say. Finally being escorted into a small room, I waited patiently as I watched patients walk by glancing in. I was really uncomfortable to say the least. My only experience with this type of unit was watching the movie *One Flew Over the Cuckoo's Nest*. So to say that I was ignorant hardly scratches the surface. Finally though, Kelli entered the room. Wearing pajamas, looking like she hadn't slept all night. She sat down across the table and began sobbing, begging me to sign her out. I was right, she hadn't slept and she was scared to death. She said that male patients were constantly making overt sexual passes at her. She was upset because she couldn't go outside to smoke. "I don't belong here. Save me." She promised me over and over again that she would stop taking the pills and that she would seek treatment right away on an outpatient basis, outside of the VA. She pleaded with me and I gave in. Yes, that's right, I caved and signed her out. And just like that, not even forty-eight hours later, she was coming back home. However, I did find solace in knowing that surely the VA would stop sending the meds after her admission into their facility. But I was wrong, they didn't. **Over the next year, over five thousand Klonopin were dispensed to Kelli. Five thousand**. In my opinion, she never stood a chance. Of course nobody was forcing the pills down her throat. I get that. But when you've become physically and emotionally dependent on a substance, regardless of what it is, constant exposure to it makes it almost impossible to resist. Especially when doctors are telling you that you need it.

20
MOVING

Kelli again became depressed, withdrawn, aggressive, and sometimes paranoid. Living with her became nearly impossible. Thomas had to stop letting her work at his tackle shop which tore him up, too. Her skin became yellowish, the whites of her eyes almost golden. It was heartbreaking.

This time I drove to the VA with Maureen in tow and stormed into the Chief of Staff's office. Maureen tried stopping me as I ambushed my way in but she couldn't. The secretary informed me that I needed an appointment but I insisted otherwise. The Chief overheard our conversation and agreed to meet with me. I tossed a bag of empty pill bottles in front of him and educated him on what was happening. I made him aware that his doctors were, from my view, killing my sister. He assured me that he was going to call a meeting with Kelli's team of doctors, which per her records that I have reviewed, he did do. Our meeting; however, was not documented. And the dispensing of pills continued. One hundred and twenty Valium and sixty Klonopin were dispensed in just one day!

I was forced to make one of the hardest decisions of my life. I sold our house. A house that we had loved. It was our home. I just couldn't bear to watch her die in it. In front of me. Watching 'us' disappear anymore. I felt helpless. I remember standing in the kitchen alone for the last time. It was empty with only the memories I would carry for us. I couldn't reach her. I didn't want it this way. I wanted my Kel back. I stared into the space recollecting the good times; Kelli on top of the refrigerator patiently waiting for the first wayward passerby to cross in front of her. She would leap off and jokingly scare the daylights out of them. I could smell the eggs and bacon that we fried up on Sunday mornings before game time. I could taste the Navy black coffee that we would sit around and drink as we plotted out our day. I missed her, *I missed you. Do you know how much? Do you Kelli*? Locking our home for the last time hurt. It was utter anguish.

I moved to an apartment in Virginia Beach while Kelli to Newport News. We were now living about thirty minutes away from each other. A distance that felt much further. Fortunately, Kelli had a roommate that would keep me updated daily. Unfortunately, Kelli was sliding. Even though she and I weren't living under the same roof anymore, I was constantly plugged into what was going on. My mind constantly occupied with simultaneous worry and hope. It was pure torture.

21
UNCERTAIN FUTURE

Kelli continued to spiral out of control as the list of medications she was taking grew. She did eventually move to an apartment closer to me in Virginia Beach which made it easier, at least for me. Most of her days were spent sleeping. She was rarely showering, her hair was greasy, and clothes unkempt. Her apartment was a disaster. Dirty laundry was just thrown everywhere, in all the rooms, including the kitchen. It constantly piled up. It was like a disturbing metaphor of stuff in the way of Kelli.

I began writing as an outlet for my stress. I taught myself how to format screenplays by reading how-to books and online articles. Following the success of the movie *Good Will Hunting* came Project Greenlight. It was a screenwriting contest being held by Matt Damon and Ben Affleck. It gave me something to concentrate on and I wrote tirelessly, learning as I went along. I wrote the screenplay *Petty Officer Grasso*, which was very loosely based on me and Kelli's Navy days. The software that I had purchased was less than fair so grammatically it was terrible. But story wise, it was different from the conventional and somewhat humorous. At least I thought so. *And I know you did to, Kelli. Even though you weren't out of the woods yet, you were with me the whole way. The Kelli I knew and have always loved.* I found temporary relief by locking myself in my room and writing. It was a short lived escape from obsessing over what Kelli was doing or whether or not she was okay. Because in the writing, it was Kelli.

I also enrolled into college, entering a Respiratory Therapy Program (leaving Coca Cola). I was a fulltime student still having a passion for taking care of patients, something that I just couldn't shake. My plan was to obtain a degree that would pay my bills once I moved out to Los Angeles to pursue acting. I was still taking acting classes and also doing some re-enactment television shows which helped to pay my rent.

The day came though where I couldn't bear it anymore and began making phone calls. I was begging for advice and in the process educating myself on the Virginia mental health system. I really had no idea where to begin or how to navigate through it. Kelli needed some help whether she wanted it or not. *I know you wanted it. I know you were in there.* I was petrified for her and truthfully just as scared for me if I had lost her. I couldn't see myself coping. Losing her simply wasn't an option.

I learned that in order to have Kelli admitted against her will I had to travel to the magistrate's office and convince him that Kelli was in danger of harming herself. And prove that she wasn't able to safely live alone any longer. Straightforward? Nope. I finally found his office after driving down every dead end street in Virginia Beach. There wasn't the luxury of a GPS back then. It took me every bit of an hour and a half. And I know that doesn't seem like a long time but when you have a loved one who was in the shape that Kelli was in, who has disappeared under the layers of a chemical veil, every second counted.

Kelli had become disoriented, confused, and incoherent. As I sat in front of the magistrate, I was broken, stressed out, and desperate. I pleaded with him as he listened, stone-faced. I had no idea what he was thinking or whether he even believed what I was saying, but still I continued on. After I was finished with my pleading speech he began questioning me as if I embellished the truth. I was enraged. But now years later, I realize that he was just doing his job. Having to play the devil's advocate. In the end though, he signed the Temporary Detention Order (TDO) which next meant that I had to go home and just wait. Something that I wasn't good at. I learned that the police would be going to pick Kelli up, and once they did they would call me. That hurled me into a very low place, a deep ugly darkness. I sat on the edge of my bed hyperventilating at the idea of Kelli sitting in the back of a police car. She wasn't a criminal. She was my twin sister. My better half.

Kelli was taken to The Virginia Beach Psychiatric Center. This ended up being the first of eleven admissions over the next decade, in addition to more in other hospitals. We were twenty-eight years old, a far stretch from the young girls headed to boot camp nearly ten years earlier to the day.

Kelli's chief complaint upon admission, "My sister who is a hypocrite put me here." Kelli hated me for having her locked up. She was furious. It shattered me that Kelli was mad at me, but I knew that it wasn't her. It was the medications. The next morning though, when her head was clearer, she called me. She needed me to bring in some of her belongings and leave them at the front desk. I brought her cigarettes, long socks, shoes without shoe strings, and sweat pants without a draw string. Over the years, I got really good at this, knowing exactly what Kelli could and could not have.

After learning that they were going to discharge Kelli after just a couple of days, I fought viciously to stop it. Two or three days were not enough, not even close, but sadly, this is how the Virginia system works. I asked my parents to come into town to participate in a hearing with me. Our job was to convince a judge that discharging Kelli to the privacy of her own home was unsafe. And we had to do this in front of Kelli, as Kelli watched, in a small room filled with people. It was awful. She stared at the table in front of her, teary eyed, as my mom and I sobbed. Kelli looked defeated, torn, and deeply hurt. I can't imagine what it was like to have your own family sitting there saying things about you that were beyond unpleasant and extremely embarrassing. My heart broke for her.

The judge ended up deciding that Kelli did in fact need more observation. But she would be sent to Salem, Virginia. Further away. It destroyed me. But in the end, I was just relieved that Kelli was going to be safe with professionals watching over her. At least for a little while longer. And just like that we were saying goodbye.

22
HELLO AGAIN

I went right back into detective mode. I searched, found, and destroyed stacks of pill bottles, cleaned Kelli's apartment, did her laundry, and decompressed. Every day I would swing by her place to get her mail and handle the bills. She began calling me several times a day. We spent most of our calls crying. We missed each other terribly and Kelli was really scared. She felt out of place in Salem. She was physically petite and felt intimidated by the other patients that accompanied her. She attended the groups but for the most part kept to herself.

She was finally discharged after ten days. She went to Pittsburgh for a little while but was excited to return home to Virginia. And I couldn't wait. When she came home, she and I hadn't missed a beat. We hung out, talked, and shook our heads at what had happened. She tried explaining to me how the pills would distort her thought processes in crazy ways. I was intrigued but it was scary. After all, she was only a prescription away from it happening again and that constantly lingered in my head. *We are talking again Kelli. It is good. I knew you were there. Stay with me this time, please, stay.*

I actually attended an appointment at the VA hospital with Kelli. It was noted that Kelli was in good spirits, and doing well. Salem had stopped all of her meds with the exception of just two antidepressants. She was no longer on benzodiazepines and narcotics. Kelli again saw the VA a couple of times after that. Her VA doctor began a trial of Seroquel which is an anti-psychotic. He prescribed it for anxiety and sleep, something that I would learn down the road was considered off-label prescribing. Kelli was neither schizophrenic nor bipolar which is what Seroquel is primarily prescribed for. As a matter of fact, on that day, it was clearly noted in her chart that she is pleasant, cooperative, alert and doing well in college. The same doctor then increased her trial from 25mg to 200mg, and threw in some Valium which was one of the drugs that Kelli was addicted too previously. It's even noted on this day that Kelli was still in college, pleasant, cooperative, and says she's staying clean and sober. But he prescribed the meds nonetheless.

Fortunately, Kelli remained determined to keep on the right track and ended up weaning herself off of the meds. Even terminating the Seroquel on her own. Yep, I had my Kelli back!

23
CAPTAIN KELLI

After Kelli returned home we carried on as if nothing had happened. Kelli moved to an apartment five minutes up the road from me and we saw each other regularly. Granted, I was still in college, auditioning for roles and taking acting classes, but we saw each other as much as possible even if that meant just visiting for a few minutes. We even took a Public Speaking class together that proved to be hilarious. Kelli hated having attention drawn to her so I took great pleasure in playing 'intently staring' spectator as she spoke in front of the classroom. She was also taking other college courses and was hopeful for a positive future. Make no mistake about it though, what happened in the past few years constantly lingered in my mind. There were times when she wouldn't answer the phone and I'd panic. Or if her apartment was less than perfect, I'd become suspicious. I was petrified that what had happened before would repeat itself.

I feel compelled to reiterate that Kelli chose to stop the Seroquel. She was as close to herself as I'd seen her in a long time. Kelli was not hospitalized at all. Life felt placid and real again. I had a lot of great friends that I met in Respiratory Therapy School, including Shannon Gillespie who embraced Kelli just as everyone else did. That's the Kelli thing. When people met her they immediately loved her. Shannon and Maureen threw Kelli and me a surprise 30th birthday party. I never dreamed so many people could pile into a small apartment like mine, but they did. And things got crazy once the male stripper showed up. I have a telling picture of Kelli and me hanging from his arms. We laughed incessantly for the entire party. I really couldn't have planned a better way of celebrating our 30th and the sweetest part of that day was having my sister there to celebrate a milestone birthday. Which is how twins are supposed to celebrate their birthdays, together.

Things got even better once Kelli purchased a boat. I can't remember exactly how long it was but it could easily fit six of us comfortably. Neither me nor Kelli knew what we were doing and had no business handling a boat in the open waters let alone the ocean or bay, but as we always did, we pushed the limits anyway. There was a day though where things got a little dangerous and frankly, quite stupid. The day started off great. We launched from Shore Drive, headed into the Chesapeake Bay, found our spot and caught a load of flounder. But then the weather changed. The sky was fiercely ticked off. We pulled the anchor and hightailed it back towards the boat ramp. For whatever reason though, we started taking on some water and I seriously thought that we were going to die that day. I really did. And then I turned my fear into anger and was enraged with Kelli, blaming her for our demise. After all, she was the Captain and our ship was sinking. 'Death by Drowning' is what my death certificate would have read. Four girls were hyper-panicked, but by the grace of God, we made it back to the ramp. Lucky for us, the ramp was full of guys that were more than willing to save us. I never got back on that boat again and neither did Kelli. She ended up selling it within a few weeks.

24
DONOR INSEMINATION

When I graduated from Respiratory Therapy (RT) school my parents came in for the big night and Kelli was thrilled for me, too. Kelli was never covetous or bitter of my small successes, whether it was my schooling, acting etc. Instead, she was genuinely happy for me and proud of my perseverance. That was just another Kelli thing. She was a booster and a role model. *You were you know.* I almost didn't finish RT School, nearly quitting early on. I had reached a breaking point emotionally having just gone through one of Kelli's breakdowns. I went to one of my instructors in tears and proceeded to tell her that I couldn't handle the stress with everything going on between Kelli and school and that I had to quit the program. But instead of just saying okay as she could have easily done, she instead reminded me that quitting would in no way, shape, or form, position me to help Kelli in the future. That instructor talked to me for a long time that day and to this very moment I'm so grateful for her words of encouragement. She stopped me from making one of the worst decisions of my life.

There were so many opportunities for Kelli to laugh off the acting thing but she never did. She watched me work hard, attending audition after audition, reading and studying the business. I would learn later after reading her journal that she was down on herself because of my small achievements, but in no way down on me. And I knew that no matter what she would root me on.

I already had some real estate brochures sent to me from California, anticipating a move out there after graduation. I even had a printed job application from Cedars-Sinai Hospital in Los Angeles. Everything was working out just as planned. I passed my registry exams and took a job at a local trauma center hoping to obtain some clinical experience before making my move, knowing that it would make me more marketable. Kelli continued in school and on the weekends we usually hit the beach or indulged at our favorite seafood restaurant, Captain George's.

After turning thirty I began having the desire to become a mom. It completely came out of nowhere. Surprising me just as much as it did Kelli. Before then having dogs was enough. I had absolutely, positively, unequivocally no desire to have children whatsoever. But one morning I woke up and thought, "I need more." I wanted to experience what so many of my friends claimed was the greatest love in existence, a child's love.

But my situation was not a conventional one. I didn't have a husband or a male partner which meant that I had to do things a little differently. I began researching artificial insemination, amongst other options. Kelli was ecstatic, hoping that she would eventually earn the title "The Most Awesome Aunt Kelli." I went to The Jones Institute in Norfolk, VA, and began the process of donor insemination. Each month was mentally, physically, and financially challenging; calculating ovulation, flip-flopping my work schedule, and struggling to afford the process all together. I tried unsuccessfully for several months; laboring through a battery of blood tests, ovulation predictor kits, pregnancy tests, fertility drugs, a hysterosalpingogram, a laparoscopy, ultrasounds etc. I was diagnosed with severe endometriosis which makes getting pregnant shall we say, tricky.

Anyone that's gone through the process of trying to get pregnant, whether conventional or not, knows how psychologically testing it is as well. I felt like a complete failure as a woman. After all, I was timing everything right. I had the best resources available helping me and it still wasn't working. Hindsight being 20/20 I'm sure the constant worry and outside stresses didn't help, and truth be told, it was a good thing that I didn't get pregnant because Kelli's mental health would soon plummet once again.

25
FOUR DIGITS

About a year passed before Kelli began acting paranoid again and lashing out at me, certain that I was against her. She was convinced that her phone was bugged and both the FBI and CIA were plotting against her. She believed she was a target of a government conspiracy. Even writing about this now, several years later, breaks my heart. *Kelli, you were free, you did it. Why did you go back, disappear, leaving me, leaving us again?*

To have someone that you love break free from the grips of a chemically induced psychosis, just to have them pulled back in again is awful. I had to once again seek a Temporary Detention Order to have Kelli admitted to Virginia Beach Psychiatric Center. This would be the first of six admissions, just this year. Kelli had wasted away to almost nothing, being the tiniest I had ever seen her. She was taking Adderall. A drug that I learned could wreak total havoc on a healthy mind. To an individual without ADHD, Adderall is simply speed throwing them into overdrive, causing sleeplessness, and a lack of appetite. Eventually leading to psychosis. Kelli did not suffer from ADHD. She just wanted to have more energy, being ignorant to the addictive nature of amphetamines.

This was an absolutely terrible year for the both of us. My dreams of moving to California ended. There was nothing that would have pulled me away from Kelli. She needed me just as I needed her so many times before. Sparing the details of each and every admission, I will sum things up. Each admission, whether voluntary or not, we would abide by the same routine. Kelli would get checked in, stabilized, and would then call me from the unit's pay phone. She had a four digit code assigned to her and unless I had that number, I wouldn't be able to call her. They simply pretended that she didn't exist, if you requested her by name without those four digits. I would anxiously await her calls while I searched her place looking for pill bottles. I would then clean up making sure that it looked perfect for when she came home. The same routine; wash her laundry, dust the furniture, shine the kitchen, and throw away the trash. I would essentially perform a Spring cleaning each and every time. And every time we talked she would tell me what she needed in the ward. It was usually socks, cigarettes, sweats, shoes, and sweat shirts. I'd throw in some pictures and gum as well. I tried making things as comfortable as possible for her which made me feel less guilty for having her put there in the first place. I would visit with her during the allotted times which were always very short, too short. We usually sat across from each other while she discretely pointed out patients, telling me their stories. Kelli never felt like she fit in there. Always being extremely uncomfortable. But patients would gravitate towards her. They trusted her. And when I walked into the unit we would get surrounded. Patients were mesmerized at how much we looked alike.

Kelli and I didn't always have the best of visits though and the stress of the entire process was emotionally and physically crushing at times. I had a full time job that required me to be mentally sharp and juggling all of this became crippling at times. And sleeping at night was hard for me too, just as it was for Kelli. The thought of her sleeping at that strange place with large, oversized doors keeping her imprisoned, tormented me. I hated every second of it. And the thought of what was coming next tormented me even more. I was constantly tired, stressed, sad, anxious and tense, trying to stay on the defensive, ready for what would come next. The reality was, and still is, when a person is admitted to a facility like the Virginia Beach Psych, it's only for a few days at the most. So although you can find temporary relief in knowing that your loved one is safe, you're forced to think about three-to-five-days from now. So there's never really any sigh of relief, ever. When visiting hours would end, I'd sit in my car and just stare up at the windows of that large, whitish/grey, gloomy building. I would wonder if Kelli was looking down at me. I hoped she was. I missed her deeply and I wanted her to feel that. The words I love you foolishly never came out of my mouth to Kelli or hers to me, but during those moments in my car, or panicking next to her on the floor while she seized, or the nights that I laid awake crying, or the all-nighters next to her gurney in the emergency room as she laid sedated, I repeated those words constantly, hoping Kelli would somehow hear me. God, I wish I said those words out loud to her while she could heard me. *I love you Kelli. Do you hear me? I know you do. I can feel it. You are always with me.*

After the last admission, Kelli voluntarily enrolled herself into an outpatient treatment program, which I was thrilled about, although obviously still guarded. And oddly enough the stupid meds that were still being dispensed to Kelli forced me to remain guarded over the years. Kelli began attending support groups at night as well. She was doing everything she could on her end to fight the disease of addiction. The "Serenity Prayer" became her favorite verse, she absolutely loved it.

God grant me the serenity
To accept the things I cannot change;

Courage to change the things I can;
And wisdom to know the difference.
Living one day at a time;
Enjoying one moment at a time;
Accepting hardships as the pathway to peace;
Taking, as He did, this sinful world
As it is, not as I would have it;
Trusting that He will make all things right
If I surrender to His Will;
That I may be reasonably happy in this life
And supremely happy with Him
Forever in the next.
Amen. (Reinhold Niebuhr)

But what Kelli couldn't control is what the medications were doing. The chemicals, slowly over the years were changing her brain chemistry, overtly evident through intermittent psychosis, paranoia, aggression, memory lapse, and suicidal tendencies.

26
BABY DANGEROUS

Kelli continued to fight for sobriety and balance, doing the best that she could. Kelli was always a warrior; after all, having me as a weak twin forced her to be. She had a sponsor and attended meetings at night determined to revisit her once confident and successful self. But her self esteem was at its lowest. The medications had taken their toll and still were at the reigns, but she continued to wrestle the ugliness, never conceding.

I was in a solid relationship and still had not given up on the notion of being a mom. I began the process of artificial insemination all over again. I tried for months unsuccessfully. When I went in for my last attempt, I decided that I had enough. I was too emotionally exhausted to continue on and frankly the process wasn't cheap. IVF wasn't an option because I couldn't afford it so after this last insemination attempt, I was throwing in the towel. But by the grace of God it worked! I'll never forget looking at the pregnancy test and seeing a pink (+) sign. I tested myself two more times immediately after because I couldn't believe the first one. After all, in my self-doubting, self-sabotaging ways, this couldn't be correct. I was beyond thrilled, running around the house senselessly. I was going to be a mom!

I hadn't told Kelli that I was actively trying because it felt like there was more pressure when people knew, so I kept it to myself. But I couldn't wait to call her. I stood in front of the fireplace holding the pregnancy test. I intently gazed at it to make sure that it didn't all of a sudden turn (-) while I dialed. I remember hoping that she answered the phone on the first ring. And she did, she answered right away. "Kel, I'm pregnant!" She was beyond elated. She knew how badly I wanted to have a baby and then screamed "We're having a baby!" And of course she wanted to scream it from the roof tops but I stopped her. I knew instantly that I couldn't tell anyone other than a few people until after the first trimester. She immediately began buying the baby little things here and there. She was so excited.

My pregnancy was a huge sigh of relief in so many ways. We could now concentrate on a positive thing, a new baby. And as my pregnancy days passed, Kelli's anticipation of becoming an aunt grew. She couldn't wait. She painted the baby's bedroom, helped me put things together, and supported me throughout the entire process. We were constantly kicking around baby names, envisioning a future of tee ball games which Kelli dreamed of coaching, and visualizing my son's first fishing trip with Kelli teaching him how to cast his rod. She was there during my first ultrasound, helped to plan the baby shower, and constantly checked in with me, making sure that I was okay. It was Kelli to the core. *Kelli, you were awesome.*

My due date was September 31st but during a meeting on September 19th I started having intense labor pains. I was actually in a meeting at the hospital that I was set to deliver in. So after kindly excusing myself, I exited the meeting and stormed into Labor and Delivery. They monitored my contractions for a little while but then sent me home. I called Kelli on my way home sharing what was happening. She planned to stay glued to her phone awaiting the big call. I gutted through the pain the best I could, showering, shaving my legs, and packing my bag. I always thought that I had a high tolerance for pain until I started having contractions. They suck. End of story. But as the evening progressed so did my pain and off to the hospital we went.

We checked in around eight o'clock. We were placed in a small room for hours before eventually getting admitted into a larger delivery room, which meant no epidural until after two o'clock in the morning. It was complete misery, but once I had the epidural, labor pains were a piece of cake. Nurses would check in on me throughout the night and doctors would check to see if I was dilating. I was four centimeters dilated by morning, but not progressing. But hey, I didn't care, I had an epidural and it was working fantastically. At the start of the morning shift my new nurse came in to introduce herself. She was extremely nice, but after looking at the baby's heartbeat monitor became concerned. And before you knew it, my room was filled with strangers. An oxygen mask was slapped onto my face, a hair net was placed onto my head, and I was rushed off to the operating room. I thought I was dying. I really thought this was the end for me.

On the way to the operating room, the anesthesiologist explained that my baby's heart rate was too low and that I needed to have an emergency C-section. Instantly my post-epidural elation vanished and fear took over. I asked Denise to call Kelli. At 8:23 a.m. I gave birth to a beautiful baby boy. By the time he was delivered, I was exhausted, medicinally intoxicated, and nauseous. They let me see him briefly before sweeping him away.

As I was being wheeled back to my room feeling foggy and blurred, I saw Kelli walking towards me. She looked scared not knowing what to say. I looked sickly with yellow skin, swollen extremities, and gray lips. She nervously waved and I smiled, slowly waving back. I was so relieved that she was there. She whispered to me that she saw my baby and evident by her smile, she was already in love with him. I decided on the name Brady, a name that I had always loved from years of watching "Days of Our Lives." Kelli chose the middle name Cole, in honor of the Navy ship that suffered a terrorist bombing years' earlier. So it was official, Brady Cole Grese would become my baby's name.

Kelli was smitten with Brady, constantly visiting him, calling me to check in on him and gloating to her friends about how cute he was. She would glowingly say, "I love that baby!" And I genuinely believe that Kelli loved Brady just as much as I did, if not more. She would joke that he was hers, too and I never argued it. When Kelli would come by the house to visit we would sit in the living room and play with Brady. She would look at him with incredible astonishment, mentally noting his every movement, coo, and whimper. And as Brady grew older, his adoration for Kelli became undeniable. When he saw her, his excitement was colossal. He had the cutest laugh as she approached him, having her wrapped around his little finger every time, all the time. Once Brady became mobile, he climbed like a monkey and leaped like a leopard, which would make Kelli awkwardly anxious. I would laugh hysterically as Kelli chased him through the living room as he vaulted from the couch to the ottoman and back to the couch again. She nicknamed him "Baby Dangerous."

I always kept a watchful eye though, knowing that Kelli was still struggling. *I had to Kelli. I know you loved him more than life itself. But it was what it was*. She made a great effort in appearing sturdy and gathered but I knew her on a level that no one else could and I sensed that things just weren't right. I knew what to look for, the so called red flags. I could pick out all the alarming behaviors. Kelli was still taking a collection of medications from the Veterans Affairs Hospital and her demeanor at times made it obvious. She tried hard to camouflage the effects of the drugs but the weight loss from the amphetamines, the sacs under her eyes from the insomnia, and her low spirits were unequivocally obvious.

I convinced Kelli to check herself back into Virginia Beach Psych. She was severely depressed and having suicidal thoughts, even writing me a note, one that I never read. I should have read that note. What was I thinking? She was also returning to the paranoia, convinced that the CIA was tracking her daily activities. She spent five days in the hospital.

I remember completely surrendering to the idea that my sister, the once heroic, durable, and gutsy half of us, was different now. It was my turn to take care of her, dodging what curve balls were thrown. Regardless of the situation, Kelli and I would walk together into the very unpredictable future; shoulder to shoulder, we would walk together. Kelli was still brave, though. Probably even braver than ever before, but the difference this time...she didn't believe it.

27
SEPSIS

Rumors ran rampant that a film was getting ready to cast in Hampton Roads, *Atlantis Down*. I found out that a friend of mine (Ethan) was the Associate Producer. We met for lunch. I picked his brain, anxiously hoping that one of the roles would fit my profile. Mary Bishop, one of the leads, was tailor made for my prior military, brunette, Caucasian, female profile. He explained that Max Bartoli was coming in from Los Angeles and that we would meet again. In the end, I read for the part and was cast as Mary Bishop. I was beyond myself. Living in Virginia obviously limits an actor/actress to less than optimal job opportunities, so to have a major film come into the area was a big deal. Especially when major players like Dean Haglund from *The X-Files* and Michael Rooker from *The Walking Dead* were already secured. Needless to say, it was exciting, and Kelli was absolutely ecstatic for me. As I said earlier, Kelli was my biggest cheerleader never once heckling my aspirations to act. Filming was set to take place in December, mostly in Virginia Beach and Portsmouth. Locations were already scouted and everything was on target.

Unexpectedly, I had to undergo a minor outpatient operation. It was a Uterine Ablation, something that would lessen the cramping associated with Endometriosis. The operation went on without a hitch, returning me home to rest on the very same day. But less than forty-eight hours later problems arose. I began having high temperatures, the highest peaking at 104.5 degrees Fahrenheit. I was also nauseous, dizzy, and in a lot of pain. Being medically inclined, I knew immediately that the high temps could prove deadly, something more serious was going on. Not wanting to wake Brady in the middle of the night, I decided that calling an ambulance was the best option. I asked them to please refrain from using their lights and sirens, cringing at the idea that the neighbors would see me looking the worst I've ever looked. I'll admit that I'm extremely vain and as I get older the vanity just seems to heighten. I'm the girl who has her lipstick on at all times, something that Kelli would say is ridiculous. Anyway, rescue came, loaded me up and off I went, convinced once again that I was dying. Horizontal in the back of the ambulance, I remember indulging in self-pity. I couldn't believe that filming was less than a couple months away and now I was going to die. That didn't seem very fair.

After being checked in to the emergency room, it was determined that I was septic. In lay terms, it meant that poison was pulsating through my veins. Working in the ICU, I had witnessed a fair number of patients die from sepsis so I knew that if it wasn't treated rapidly it could kill me. My temperature was sky high and my blood pressure dangerously low, calling for immediate IV antibiotics. I was shuffled to a room that was no bigger than my clothes closet. I'm not exaggerating here. The rooms at this particular hospital are very small but as sick as I was, I didn't care. Well, I should say, I didn't care during the first few days of my stay. I was admitted to the 'step-down unit' one level away from the ICU. I had worked at this hospital many times before, being floated there during staff shortages, so I knew a lot of the staff which made me extremely anxious. Vanity proved problematic again, keeping my hospital room door closed at all times, fearing someone that I knew would see me. The staff there were great, even hanging a sign on the door directing everyone to the nurse's station.

The first few hours were spent having my blood drawn to identify the poison, my vital signs being monitored constantly, a revolving door of doctors, CAT scans, and phone calls from my family. I was hesitant to tell Kelli though, not wanting to thrust her into an even worse place than she already was. But I had too. I needed her there. With me. The first day that I was there though I told her not to come because I was just too sick. And a part of me was rather nervous because I didn't know how Kelli would be. I never really knew what to expect with Kelli's emotional stability at that point and I was scared that Kelli would show up a little off, which would just stress me out even more.

The initial night there turned disastrous, suddenly being awakened by uncontrollable shivering. My bed was soaked from sweat feeling as though someone threw a bucket of water over it. My nurse rushed in calling others for support. I pleaded with her to not call for help using the overhead speaker because I knew that my coworkers would know that it was me having problems. She kindly obliged and started calling doctors with her cell phone. I remember being terrified, absolutely terrified. Honestly, the rest of that night is a blur for me with the exception of one thing. I mustered enough energy to record a video onto my laptop with the built-in web cam. I ended up deleting it months later not being able to watch it. I was convinced that first night that I needed to say goodbye to my son if in fact I didn't beat the sepsis.

I woke up the next morning feeling the sickest I'd ever felt. Kelli came in around 11, tiptoeing nervously. She wasn't sure what to expect and fear was written all over her face. I did my best to console her despite that I was extremely pale and physically beaten down. She sat in the chair next to me. The only other piece of furniture that could fit in the room. She and I hardly spoke. I was too sick and she was too scared. She watched the nurses come in throughout the day changing the bags on my continuously transfusing IV. I found out that I had two dangerous venoms, E. coli and Enterococcus. I was shocked, completely stunned. I mean, after all, why in the world would I have E. coli poisoning? Either way though, that's what I had. The bacteria were taking over my bloodstream and my physicians were shaking their heads confusingly which scared me even more. Kelli was petrified, at times just whispering my vital signs to mom on the phone, oblivious to my eavesdropping.

For days, every morning Kelli would call asking me what I needed before showing up around eleven o'clock. She would set up shop in her chair and we'd watch television for hours. Kelli and I both loved reality shows and I remember a marathon of Antonio Sabato Junior's show airing one day. I don't even recall the name of it, but in short, he was trying to find a wife. Kelli and I watched that show for hours, enjoying every second of the drama-filled spectacle.

I kept the *Atlantis Down* script next to me, in the nightstand drawer. Every once in a while, Kelli would ask me if I wanted to run lines but usually I was too sick to care. I did try though at night, when I was alone. I was nervous that my role would be recast, adding to my anxiety and the walls began smothering me, inducing depression and pessimism. Those days were challenging, testing a part of me that's never been tested. I had no control of the situation, relying solely on antibiotics that would hopefully head off any more problems. The Enterococcus was affecting my heart, which in turn, was causing my low blood pressure. I felt helpless. And this time, Kelli couldn't save me either.

I was given the option of going home, contingent on having a PICC line inserted, which was basically an IV that granted access directly to my heart. Home care nursing would be established since I had to continue with the aggressive antibiotic therapy. Even though I was feeling defeated, I agreed. Going home to my son with a huge needle submerged in my arm nearly broke me. Thinking back to those days, I should have just been relieved to go home; but when you're going through something so traumatic, your brain works a little differently.

When Kelli drove me home I was depressed, tired, and moody. After days in that small room it began wearing on my psyche. I had Kelli swing me by the drugstore before returning to the house. We filled my prescriptions and purchased a portable blood pressure monitor. I was still extremely nervous because my blood pressure, even at discharge, was very low. After spending some time with Brady, I spent the rest of the time in bed. I wasn't myself and still felt shell-shocked from everything.

Three days later, I ended up back in the emergency room with severe diarrhea and fevers. The antibiotics were taking their toll. I was again admitted to another small, depressing room. I ended up spending six more days hospitalized and grim. The sepsis ended up resolving itself, but the experience was humbling to say the least.

Following my recovery, we filmed *Atlantis Down* in just two weeks which was considered extraordinary by most for a full length feature. The days were exceedingly long, as most shoots are. Kelli was on set every day and for that I am eternally grateful. I was thrilled that she could experience it with me. I was following my passion and seriously thought this might not happen because of the sepsis. She was endlessly snapping pictures. Those two weeks of filming will forever own a special place in my heart not only because it was a great set to work on, but because Kelli was there – showing so much support despite her own struggles.

28
SEROQUEL

Kelli voluntarily admitted herself into the hospital, again. One of her chief complaints was "I'm so agitated, lifeless, I'm basically hooked on pills. My health and my mind are shot." It shattered my heart when I read those words (in her journal) after losing her. If only I had asked more questions. If only I had stormed into the VA again. If only I had known that they began prescribing her Klonopin again. If only I had screamed from the mountain tops a little louder. If only. The VA had just dispensed another sixty Klonopin. And of course Kelli was still taking the Seroquel, the anti-psychotic that I pleaded for Kelli to stop taking. But Kelli couldn't, she depended on its sedating effects to sleep, unable to give it up. Again, as I write this, I'm tempted to rehash medications, quantities, and possible side effects, but I'm going to resist this frustration.

During this particular admission Kelli felt really defeated. She was sad, anxious, and overcome with self-loathing. She was ashamed, feeling conquered by the grasp of medications and remedies that her physicians felt she needed. Her general appearance was described as tearful and weepy, something that describes me now as I type these words. She was depressed, not able to care for herself any longer, letting her living conditions decline, again. But as she always did, she worked hard, attending group discussions and trying to stabilize.

Kelli was set to be discharged the same day that our Grandma Sorrentino passed away. I phoned the hospital requesting a conference call with Kelli and a social worker. I needed to make sure that Kelli wasn't blindsided once she returned home. Something that could shatter her recovery. I dreaded that phone call, unsure of what to expect. Kelli and I had always been close to our grandparents and I knew that it would hit hard for her. The social worker called me with Kelli in the room on speaker. After a quick introduction the stage was turned over to me. I remember Kelli's voice greeting me nervously. Most likely expecting me to discuss my concerns about her. I gently broke the news to Kelli explaining that we have to travel to Pittsburgh for the funeral. At first I heard silence, but then Kelli began to sob. I was glad that I chose to tell Kelli the way that I did, giving her an opportunity to digest our grandma's death with someone safe by her side. Kelli opted to fly home while I would drive. Kelli wanted some time to return to her condo, pack some bags, and prep for the unfortunate trip home which made complete sense. And I was okay with that because Kelli really did seem to be in a good place. Showing positive and optimistic thoughts for a better future and she was thrilled to see Brady again. Little did I know though that Kelli had plans of calling the VA that very same day requesting a refill of Seroquel. They dispensed her 540 Seroquel, 120 Phenobarbital, and Tramadol all through a phone consult on that same afternoon.

Kelli flew in the following morning quiet and reserved. She was processing a lot. Obviously still on an enormous amount of medications that I wasn't aware of at the time. Our grandmother's service was held in a chapel on cemetery grounds close to the grave site. During the service, Kelli and I each sat next to our mom, one on each side. Our mom was devastated, just losing our grandfather not too long before. The three of us plotted to discretely stay behind after the service, hoping to observe our grandmother's casket descending into the earth. After the service, we drove down to the site where the casket was already unloaded. It was dangling over its final resting place next to our grandfather's. We stood at the top of the hill watching as the groundsmen, aware of our presence, carefully lowered the casket. We sobbed as we witnessed what we were told we couldn't. That was a special moment that we shared with our mom amongst many others. We spent the next few days reminiscing in an almost childlike fashion, reflecting on our days with our grandmother. Our grandmother had a quirky love for bingo, a firm loyalty to her soap operas, *General Hospital* being her favorite, and she more-than-the-world loved her grandchildren.

After a few days, Kelli and I returned home to Virginia Beach. I remember being extremely anxious after dropping her off. I hated leaving her just as much as she hated me leaving. She was lonely and that was agonizing for me.

Kelli voluntarily entered a 21 day Veteran's Affairs outpatient substance abuse program. She soldiered on determined to regain control of her life, free of prescription pacifiers. Frustratingly though, I've learned since reviewing Kelli's records, that the VA continued to prescribe the very same medications that she had struggled with for so many years, even dispensing sixty Klonopin during her participation in the program.

As the medications continued, so did Kelli's emotional and physical decline. She began withdrawing, usually not answering her phone or venturing far from her home. Her visits to Brady were also diminishing. This went on for several weeks, keeping me on edge and panicky, running to the house phone in anticipation of bad news. Over the years I had received a lot of un-welcomed calls, some from emergency rooms, so I became accustomed to the unavoidable process.

Another three weeks passed and then Kelli agreed to

voluntarily check herself into the VA Hospital as a last ditch effort. And I have to point out that writing about this incident, right at this very moment, knocks the wind out of me, I can hardly catch my breath. I know that it's necessary though, so I'll push through this. I had never seen Kelli as broken as she was on this day. She had shaved half of her head, convinced that the FBI implanted a tracking device. Her condo was in complete and utter disarray, her floor covered wall to wall with dirty laundry, while her toilets overflowed with stool. She looked as if she hadn't showered or slept in days. After years of powerful, mind altering medications, it had come to this, a scene similar to a horror film movie set. Kelli's head shamefully dropped as I gasped searching for the right words, any words. I quickly noticed her embarrassment and jumped right into a joke making light of a very dark situation. We agreed that we would throw a quick load of laundry in, clean up the place, and then head straight to the hospital. Neither of her toilets were functional due to the deposits which forced me to question her. At first she was hesitant to answer but then explained that she worried that her water was poisoned, a fear that prevented her from showering or flushing. I had never been sadder before that moment, ever, in my entire life. I was crushed. Feeling so horribly heartsick for her. I found some plastic gloves and off we went, shoveling the mess, handful by handful into trash bags. She scooped and I held the bag, both of us dry-heaving. But believe it or not we were able to summon a couple of jokes as we did this unspeakable and nauseating task, turning to humor as a reservoir for sanity, as we always did in the past. We had too. Humor was always our go-to.

Moving on to Kelli's bedroom I noticed that something was strange with her bedroom wall. I looked closer realizing that she had carved J loves M into her freshly painted wall. She explained that the initials were for Jesus and Mia. That's all she would tell me.

I asked Kelli is she minded if I took some photos of her half-shaven hair and condo. I felt certain that looking at the pictures of her living conditions, the VA Hospital wouldn't be able to minimize the situation. And Kelli, being a good sport as always, agreed. We went on with our photo shoot. Kelli actually was trying to smile in a couple of shots. She did her best to maintain a brave face knowing that her situation was dire. I always envied her strength, I still do. We arrived at the VA, finally sitting down with a nurse who knew Kelli well. We sat in the small room together as Kelli explained her situation, her desire to no longer live, her delusional thoughts and her hopelessness for the future. I stepped through the digital photos on my camera leaving the nurse speechless. It sickened me to do that knowing Kelli was embarrassed, but feeling like there was no other way to truly capture the desperate crisis, I felt like I had no choice. We were then immediately passed along to a physician who asked more in-depth questions. And again I showed the photos. Kelli made it clear that if she left that facility she would in fact take her own life.

As we sat there silently, the doctor made a few phone calls. He then hesitantly informed us that the only VA Hospital that had any female beds available was in Salem, VA, which meant that Kelli and I would be separated. This devastated the both of us. Sadly, this was a common problem never making sense to either one of us. But regardless, that was the scenario and we had to deal with it. We were ushered to the waiting room, awaiting a transport team.

We sat next to each other; shoulder to shoulder, voiceless, dreading what we knew was coming. Kelli would be taken away in a small white van as I stood waving goodbye. It was distressing to us both. But if this meant saving Kelli's life then so be it.

I needed to update my mom on what was going on so I gave Kelli some money to buy us a couple of coffees from Starbucks that was just diagonal from the chairs we were sitting in. Reassuring her that I'd be back in ten minutes, I went out to my car leaving her alone. Unbeknownst to me, Kelli had a bottle of Seroquel packed in her bag. A bag that I feel should have been searched by the nurse who checked us in knowing that Kelli was admittedly and actively suicidal. I was too distraught to even think about doing that but I wished that I had. While I was gone, Kelli swallowed that whole bottle of pills. Shortly upon my return, which was only after a few minutes, Kelli became symptomatic resulting in unconsciousness and cardiac arrhythmia. She was rushed to the emergency room while I stood frozen. I couldn't breathe. She was eventually transferred to the ICU where I sat holding her hand, something I had never done before. I nervously watched her breathing, hoping that it wouldn't become labored. She then began having seizures. Her first when it was just me in the room. I ran into the hallway screaming for help. I was fear stricken. Kelli remained unconscious for days. I prayed over her with a chaplain, decorated her room with pictures, and told her that I loved her countless times. I talked in great length with the physicians taking care of her. I wanted them to stop the Seroquel once and for all. I had learned after talking with several medical professionals that if in fact a patient is not truly psychotic due to mental illness, then taking an anti-psychotic can in fact induce psychosis. And I felt strongly that after years of these mind altering drugs, including the Seroquel, this is what was happening to Kelli. And additionally, it's also proven that these medications can increase suicidal thoughts and behaviors, something too, I believe was happening to Kelli.

While Kelli was in the ICU I began contacting medical malpractice attorneys. I wanted to stop the VA from prescribing anymore Seroquel, but knowing that this wouldn't happen simply by my request, I was hoping an attorney could help. I must have emailed and called fifteen to twenty with no luck. However one lawyer, Robert Haddad, did spend a considerable amount of time talking with me, explaining that because medical malpractice suits are so expensive to pursue, most firms only take on cases that end in tragedies such as death or some sort of life altering condition.

When Kelli woke up days later she was confused. We talked a lot once I knew she was able to comprehend what had happened. She remembered taking the Seroquel but after that, nothing. Once she was considered stable enough to transfer from the hospital, six days later, she was moved again to Virginia Beach Psych after Kelli and I pleaded that she not be transferred to Salem. And then after her release from VB Psych, the VA continued her on the Seroquel.

Kelli was again admitted into the hospital after another overdose of Seroquel. She was found the evening before by the police, unconscious in her truck. They took her to the emergency room where a temporary detaining order was eventually obtained. She ended up staying in the psych hospital for five days. Another month passed then Kelli again overdosed on Seroquel landing her in a Pennsylvanian hospital. She was visiting my parents at the time.

All of Kelli's overdoses and hospitalizations are documented in Kelli's records, even notes pointing out specifically that Kelli's overdoses were on Seroquel. Still though, the medication was continued.

It's even noted by a suicide prevention case manager that Kelli's suicide attempts were through Seroquel overdoses. The case manager also suggests in the treatment plan to limit the means. This was included within in one of the admission notes, "This note serves as a warning regarding past self-directed violence with suicidal intent and injury. Veteran overdosed in two separate events in one month's time which included large amounts of Seroquel."

Kelli chose to enroll in an inpatient program at the VA Hospital which would require her to spend most of the summer at the Domiciliary on campus. I was very proud of her thinking this was a ray of hope for us. We talked on the phone daily, and I visited often. She was anxious to get home though, eager to see Brady. And when *Atlantis Down* was scheduled to premiere at the Commodore Theater in Portsmouth, VA, Kelli wanted to get well to be there.

29
ATLANTIS DOWN

The world premiere became the talk of the town locally for weeks. Michael Rooker and Dean Haglund were both traveling in for the event which made it even more exciting for the small city of Portsmouth. It was thrilling for so many reasons, mostly though because Kelli was given permission (from her program) to attend the event. Facebook was buzzing with première updates, the local media was providing a lot of coverage, and the Commodore Theater had sold out.

My Aunt Marie and mom traveled in for the big night which sweetened the deal even more for me. A stretch limo was set to take my family and friends to the premiere which was becoming a major red carpet event. Kelli was beside herself almost as much as I was. I had a mass of friends from my hospital attending as well, over the years becoming more like family.

The moment finally arrived after weeks of anticipation and the nerves began kicking in. I was a wreck, but eager. I had worked really hard for several years to make it on to the silver screen and even though my character's life was short lived in the film, it was still a lead. And I was proud of my performance. Truthfully, making the decision to stay in Virginia for me was also accepting that the opportunity for me to walk a red carpet event was slim to none. And to most this probably seems ridiculous and insignificant, but to an aspiring actor/actress it's a big deal. It's not a career choice for the thin-skinned. It's a daunting journey.

The cast met at a local hotel awaiting our call to the theater. Each of us would arrive by limo, walk the red carpet, and interview with the media. As my limo approached the theater, Kelli appeared through the smoked-out limo windows, enthusiastically anticipating my arrival. I could see her but she couldn't see me. Her zealous expression is forever etched into my mind, a priceless flashback for me now. She looked fantastic, dressed fashionably in her black ensemble, and composed. As I walked passed her she waved and continued snapping pictures. She was as proud of me as I of her.

Once everyone was seated, Kelli's table ended up in front of mine, giving me a direct view of her expressions. As the opening credits rolled, I watched her, as if no one else was in the room. I didn't need anyone else there. I had my twin sister back. *Can we just go back, Kelli, please, to that moment*?

When my name appeared in the opening credits there was a roar from my friends. It was one of the most out of body experiences I've ever felt in my entire life. Every once in a while I'll watch the internet video clip of the premiere. In fact, you get a glimpse of Kelli waiting for me in the beginning, you see my Aunt Marie stumble out of the limo, and you hear the roar from the crowd when my name appears on screen. It was one of the most incredible experiences of my life, especially since Kelli was there.

The film played each night for that entire week with parties following. For me, everything seemed to be falling into place perfectly. Kelli seemed to be stronger, my acting career felt like it was finally picking up steam, and life just seemed a little easier.

Having a large military presence locally it only made sense to have a military night for the film. Afterward, at a local restaurant, I enjoyed a nice conversation with a Master Chief and his colleagues.

I saw Kelli several times after that week. She was always anxious to visit Brady. Most of the time we just hung out in the living room entertained by Brady's acrobats with an occasional trip to Starbucks thrown in. Kelli drank the Cappuccino, and me the Caramel Macchiato. Halloween was soon approaching and for days I asked Kelli to dress up in a costume with me but she refused. Or so I thought. To my surprise Kelli did show in costume. A Monk. Leaving me completely stunned, jaw to the floor. I ran upstairs and threw on my astronaut costume (from the film) and off we went. One of my favorite pictures of Kelli and Brady is from that night. He's looking up at her with the biggest grin and she's radiating from his unconditional love of her. That night would end up being the last time that Kelli and I were pictured together. Halloween for me now, like every other holiday and milestone, isn't the same. Never will be.

30
I'M SORRY TO INFORM YOU

I've struggled for years on how to write this down. Coming up with excuse after excuse as to why I haven't written it. I've relived this transition countless times over in my head causing me severe anxiety, punishing insomnia, and harrowing nightmares. I've learned recently that I suffer from post traumatic stress disorder caused not only by Kelli's death, but the years of struggling to keep her alive leading up to it. Truthfully, I want to avoid writing this part of the story altogether but in order to tell the entire story, as it was and still is, I have to tell this part as well.

I saw Kelli for the last time on Sunday, November 6th 2010. She came by the house to visit Brady with her new rescue dog Rocco. She was quiet, unusually quiet, and I suspected things were off with her. Her stay was brief, hanging around long enough to dote on Brady. As she was getting ready to leave, I asked her if she could pick me up on Friday morning (9 a.m.) the 12th, and drive me to and from a doctor's appointment. You see, years later, my tail bone now caused me severe pain requiring injections every six months, leaving me unable to drive after the procedure. Naturally, she said yes. She was to pick me up at nine o'clock sharp. After that, she left. We talked several times that week on the phone but working three twelve hour shifts in a row made it difficult to visit. On November 11, 2010, Veterans Day, I worked a twelve hour shift at the hospital. I was working in the burn trauma ICU that day and happened to sit down for a short break. *Oprah* was on television. She was interviewing Marie Osmond, asking about her son's suicide. Now Kelli never missed an episode of *Oprah* so I knew she was watching. Marie Osmond was discussing her coping process after her son's suicide. And I don't remember specifically what she said or how she said it but I remember thinking to myself, this is it, Kelli's going to watch this episode and then she's going to kill herself. Somehow, I felt like Kelli, after listening to Marie Osmond, would think that I could in fact survive her death without my other half. Shortly after the show ended, I grabbed my cell phone and walked down the hallway for some privacy. Kelli had tried calling me twice but I didn't carry my phone at work, but I do now, every day. Every damn day. I tried calling her back but she didn't answer. I called several times, thinking I would eventually annoy her enough to pick up but she didn't. She called Marie and my mom also. Briefly talking to each of them.

The next couple of hours at work were challenging, trying to get my mind off of Kelli. I couldn't shake it though, I just couldn't. My neighbor Suzanna was babysitting Brady so I had to go straight home, calling Kelli throughout the entire drive. Still though, there was no answer. I cried myself to sleep that night. I knew that I would never see my sister again.

The next morning, the day of my appointment, I knew that Kelli wasn't coming, she was gone. Half of me was dead. Kelli was always punctual so my plan was to wait until 9:05. I would then walk Brady next door and go to Kelli's condo. And this is exactly what I did. When I took Brady next door, Suzanna asked where Kelli was. My answer, "She's dead." These were my words, as crazy as they sounded, that's all I could say. I made two phone calls on the way over to Kelli's, one to the doctor's office and one to the Virginia Beach Police Department, asking them to meet me at Kelli's. Even though I had Kelli's spare key that she had given me, the thought of finding my sister dead mortified me.

I arrived at Kelli's condo, pulled into the parking lot, and just waited. I was reluctantly right. Kelli's black Ford Escape was still in her assigned parking space. Just a few minutes later, two police officers arrived and approached my vehicle. The male officer, with a bit of sarcasm, asked why I hadn't knocked yet or entered the condo since I had the key. And I understood why, it did sound crazy, I got it. But all I could do was hand him the key, chancing, hoping that I was completely wrong, wanting to look as idiotic as they thought that I was. There was nothing dragging me into that condo, finding my twin sister lifeless on the floor, nothing.

I watched as they walked towards the condo eventually disappearing from my line of vision, leaving me only to wait. I was praying that they would eventually wave me in with Kelli sitting on the couch regretful that she had forgotten my appointment. But instead, additional officers began showing up, including a detective in an unmarked vehicle. I was heartsick. The two officers that entered Kelli's condo still hadn't returned which was also alarming. Officers began convening on the sidewalk not far from the condo and not being able to take the anxiety of waiting any longer, I joined them. They were secretive, not answering me when I asked if Kelli was okay. I continued to pry but still no answer. I was hoping that an ambulance would show up, at least signaling that Kelli was alive. But instead, the initial two officers that went in to Kelli's condo, exited and began walking straight towards me. They were smiling as they talked with each other, obviously not seeing me yet, but when they did their faces completely changed. "Ma'am, I'm sorry to inform you that your sister is in fact deceased," the female officer softly stated. My knees buckled and my life at that very moment was changed forever. Those words forever echo in my head, haunting me. "Your sister is in fact deceased…your sister…your…" Kelli, not Kelli. No. Not Kelli!

I asked about her dog Rocco. Kelli adored him and I needed to get my hands on him, somehow to still feel a physical connection. They informed me that he was okay but shaken. Kelli had left plenty of food and water for him but he had obviously been alone for hours. When they brought him to me and handed him over, he was shivering. All I could do was hug him as tightly as I could, reassuring him that it would be okay. I held him, Kelli for a long time. He wanted 'ok' as much as I did. Animal Control arrived planning to take Rocco. I pleaded with them to give me a few days to figure things out. They agreed.

The detective asked me to come to his car as more and more people began arriving. We sat there quietly. I could hardly speak through the sobs. The pain that I felt that morning was disabling. I wanted to see Kelli but he suggested I didn't. And now, I'm glad that I listened. I did ask him specific questions that I now wish I hadn't. He asked if he could call anyone for me but I said emphatically, "No, I will handle it." I returned to my car as he went into Kelli's condo with a camera, some white bags, and gloves.

My mom was waiting for my call. She too, had a bad feeling the night before. But I couldn't get myself to call her. Instead, I called Marie and told her to go to my mom. Mom shouldn't be alone. I remember Marie's gasp as if it were yesterday. I then called Maureen, knowing she would come to Kelli's, so I wasn't there alone. She answered, wailing after I told her what had happened. She immediately came. I made several other calls while I waited for Maureen, including to Denise who was out of town, my friends Teddi and Dee, and my boss Vickie.

Shortly after Maureen had arrived, a white van pulled up. I knew right away why they were there. Two men, dressed in suits, entered Kelli's condo, pushing a stretcher. I found it impossible to wholly believe, to take to heart, that my twin sister was being taken away in a white van. Another change forever etched in my mind.

The two men eventually reappeared with Kelli covered by a blanket. They stopped in front of me, giving me an opportunity to say goodbye. I placed my hands on top of her, wishing like hell she would pop up, shouting "Gotcha!" But she didn't. She was gone, forever. I watched that van pull away knowing that half of me was in it.

The detective brought me Kelli's key, gave me his card, and left with the rest of the officers. Hesitantly, Maureen and I entered Kelli's condo. I could hardly catch my breath as I walked through the door. It still wasn't real. I immediately noticed that a few pictures were missing out of the collage picture frame that hung in her living room. A collection that I put together for her as a Christmas present. And this was an immediate clue that Kelli was experiencing paranoia again, because it's something she had done in the past. I then discovered sitting perfectly on the arm of the recliner, her favorite black hat and a half-smoked cigar placed in the ashtray with her Zippo lighter next to it. Now Kelli didn't smoke cigars, only cigarettes, so to me, it was almost like a celebration of some sort, making peace with her decision to end her life. A life that was full of torment from several years of prescribed mind altering medications. I still have that cigar, inside of the hat box, and will one day smoke the remainder once I am confident that I fulfilled my promise to Kelli; telling her story in hopes of saving lives. *Once again Kelli you will be there for others. Even in your darkest moments.*

I will travel to the Albert G. Horton Cemetery in Suffolk, VA, wearing the black hat, donning the scent of Ralph Lauren Blue (her favorite perfume), and I will smoke that cigar. *You will have finished another mission Kelli. You never left any project undone. This one is no exception. I promise you.*

I began rummaging through Kelli's belongings hoping for some sort of sign. I tore through boxes and drawers looking for a note. I never found a note but I did find a journal, addressed to me, "If found upon my death." I opened it, read a few lines, but then had to quickly close it. It was just too painful to read, you will see. In Kelli's clothes closet hung the black outfit that she wore to the film premiere, except this time, it had an angel pin fastened to the collar. That ended up being the outfit that Kelli was laid out in.

I stayed there for a few hours before opting to leave. The police had confiscated all of the medication bottles found at Kelli's condo, but I knew that the medical examiner's office would have them. I had no doubt what-so-ever that it had been the Seroquel that Kelli overdosed on, but I just needed official confirmation.

Leaving her condo was nearly impossible for me that day. As I opened her front door to leave, I turned back around, re-living thirty-eight years in a blink of an eye. My hands trembled as I locked her door. The agony deeply felt.

31
MASTER CHIEF

I couldn't get home fast enough to Brady. I needed to hug him. I needed his little arms to wrap around me, reminding me that I would be okay. I wasn't sure about how I would approach Kelli's death with him, but I knew that his embrace would bring me momentary comfort. Those first few hours were excruciating, having no idea what to do or where to begin. I literally went from the highest of highs (with the film premiere) to the lowest of lows (with Kelli…gone) and I was barely keeping it together. I couldn't stop crying. My tears were uncontrollable, confusing my poor little boy who had no clue as to what happened to his Aunt Kelli.

I called the medical examiner's office, I couldn't resist the urge. I had to find out for myself; her thoughts on what had happened to Kelli. I spoke with the doctor who kindly offered me some information. She made it clear that Kelli did in fact overdose on pills and Seroquel was the empty bottle of pills near her, likely the ones that Kelli swallowed. But of course we would have to wait for the official autopsy report to confirm this which ended up taking over three months, agonizing to say the least. After speaking to her, I hung up the phone livid.

Then my mom called, obviously grief stricken as well. Her flight was already booked. She was flying in with Marie. My mom suggested that Kelli be flown up to Pittsburgh to be buried there which sent me into more rage. I began yelling into the phone. After all of these years of being with Kelli, she was about to be ripped away from me. I hung up on my mom and immediately called a friend of mine who was a local blogger named David. I explained the situation and asked if he knew of any lawyers that could help me stop my family from taking Kelli out of the state. And within a few minutes he called back with a name and number of a lawyer that could help me at a moment's notice. Although I knew my mom was coming from a good place, no one was taking my Kelli away from me! She was already gone, and now I wouldn't be able to visit the grave. No one. Besides, this was Kelli's home now and it had been for many years. Now on the defense my stress level was off the charts. I couldn't turn my neck, my shoulders locked, too, rigid. It was not only painful, but frustrating, because I could hardly function physically, having to turn my entire body just to look in both directions. I cried myself to sleep that first night with one of Kelli's blankets. I curled in a fetal position, sobbing.

The following day, Denise and I went to the funeral home and met with Mike Strickland. His presence was large, but his voice, calming. He escorted us back to a conference room, sat us down, and paused for a moment. Once I was finally able to make eye contact with him, he said the words, "We have your sister Kelli here with us." Another etched memory. He said them in the kindest, most caring of ways but I just wanted my twin sister back. But instead, I was talking to a funeral director, planning out her funeral.

When we walked through the room that housed the caskets, I felt numb, completely disconnected from myself. I knew that Kelli wanted to be cremated but I was still weighing all the options. *I hear you Kelli, "Dar, do what makes you feel okay."* Mike then showed us the two rooms that were available for viewings. There was a blue room and a pink room. I told Mike right away that Kelli would hate the pink. We spent a lot of time with Mike that day. He's a special soul who's doing exactly what he should be doing and if it weren't for him, I'm not sure if I would have gotten through the process as I did. I decided on cremation, what Kelli originally wanted. Same 'ole Kel, knowing I would find my way to doing what she said we should do in the first place. *Well what should I do now, Kelli? Am I telling it right? I know you will be there when I go to bed. For hours we talked. Remember?*

Since Kelli was a Veteran, she was eligible for an Honor Guard team. I wanted Kelli's funeral to be as beautiful as it possibly could be, that's what she deserved. I told Mike about the Master Chief that I had met at the film premiere who happened to be a Command Master Chief. I was hoping that he could supply me with a team, which he did without hesitation. I also decided on a bagpipe player as well who would play TAPS after the service.

My mom and Marie flew in later that day. When I caught glimpse of them for the first time as they walked towards me, I felt a tremendous relief having them there. We desperately embraced. The rest of my family was driving in. The three of us went back to my place and began going through pictures for the slide show that would play during the service. There were thousands of captured memories that spanned over three decades. I never appreciated pictures as much as I do now. I also showed them Kelli's journal but they weren't emotionally ready to read it, it was just too hard. The topic of where Kelli would be buried did come up again, but thankfully it was decided that Kelli's home was here, in Virginia. Her friends were here, her home was here, and this is the place where she considered home.

The morning of the viewing was unnerving. I was petrified to see Kelli, not certain I could handle it. The drive to the funeral home was silent. None of us spoke.

When we entered the funeral home Mike met us right away at the front door. I felt like at any moment I could lose consciousness, I was so anxious and scared. He began to prepare us as best he could but I felt myself tuning him out, hoping that if I didn't hear him this nightmare would end. But it didn't. The reality was, my twin sister, the other half of me, was in that blue room, and dressed in her black suit, gone forever.

Mike led us in, my mom and me leading the way. As I approached the casket, my entire life flashed in front of me, a life that always consisted of Kelli with me. I didn't know what to do with what I was feeling. Half of me died on Veteran's Day night, alongside Kelli. Kelli looked beautiful and at peace. Mike did an amazing job with her makeup and hair, everything was exactly the way she wore it.

I took the chair closest to Kelli's face, my mom standing behind me. I touched Kelli's hand, it was cold. The room sat silent for several minutes, which was unusual for a large group like ours, but no one had anything to say, only feelings of sadness and disbelief. I felt an overwhelming feeling of failure. I couldn't wrap my head around the fact that after surviving everything that we had gone through together, the medications, the hospitalizations, the doctors, this is how it would end. Just shy of our 38th birthday, Kelli was dead.

Once catching my breath, I began sobbing, which prompted my mom to bend down and whisper in my ear, which startled me. I jumped up out of my chair screaming which in turn startled my entire family. And as crazy as this might sound, at that moment, I had thought it was Kelli's voice that I was hearing. After my mom assured me that it was just her, we actually chuckled. And Kelli, being the practical joker that she was, got the last laugh.

As friends began piling in I did my best to greet them with my still frozen neck. I looked terrible, but did my best to stay as composed as possible. Somehow, offering support to others comforted me. Kelli had a lot of friends, although sadly, she never felt like it. I remember a long moment, staring through the room full of people at Kelli's casket. It was probably twenty feet or so away from where I was standing. There was a black and gold Steelers Terrible Towel draped over the side which my Uncle Paul had strategically placed. It seemed perfect, representing Kelli's love of the Steelers. It was at that moment that I realized how truly, utterly beautiful my sister was. I wished she would have seen that in herself. She was one of the kindest, most giving, and good-hearted people that you'd ever meet. Her heart was golden.

Thomas, from the tackle shop where Kelli used to love to work, stood next to me at one point, he too, distraught. He asked about Rocco, Kelli's dog. I explained that I didn't know what to do because I couldn't keep him. All I did know is that I'd find him a good home no matter what the cost. Thomas asked if he could adopt Rocco and I was beside myself. I couldn't have thought of a better person to love Rocco, it was meant to be. Every Christmas Eve since, we go to Thomas' house to visit Rocco. We bring them both treats and take lots of pictures.

The next morning, the funeral was the hardest, being the last time I would ever lay eyes on my sister. Kelli's casket was in the front center of the room as both televisions played through the slide show. Guests, one by one, said their last goodbyes as we watched on. I sat in the front row staring at Kelli. I couldn't stop staring at her trying to memorize every detail of her face. Needing to ask Mike a question, I had to walk through the room of guests in order to get to him. And as I lifted my eyes up from the floor as much as I could, I saw Christy in the crowd which left me stunned. I hadn't seen her in several years and having her there was a true testament as to how special Kelli was.

I decided that I would read a eulogy, something that surprised most people including myself honestly. I wasn't sure if I would get through it or not but I had to try. I stumbled, but I finished. Throughout the service three songs were played. I chose "I Can Only Imagine" by Mercy Me. We also decided on "Don't Stop Believin" by Journey, one of Kelli's favorites, and "Proud to be an American" by Lee Greenwood, a song that Kelli and I both loved.

The flag that draped Kelli's casket after its final closure would be folded by the Honor Guard team that was kindly donated to me and my family. As the flag ceremony commenced, I immediately began reminiscing of the days when Kelli and I performed ceremonies. None of what was happening seemed real. Once folded, the Navy Chief took to his knee and presented the flag to my mom. And then, as Kelli's casket was slowly moving past me, I placed both of my hands on top of it, just as I did when she was removed from her condo, my heart was broken, my spirit crushed.

The ceremony continued outside, as the bagpiper began to play. Each guest was given a balloon, either black or gold, which would be released simultaneously. But as everyone began releasing, I kept mine, squeezing it to my chest, I never let it go, I couldn't.

And just when I thought it was over, the Navy Chief approached me. He was carrying another folded flag. He explained that it was a flag that was flown for twenty-four hours at the Naval Hospital where Kelli and I were once stationed in Portsmouth. He removed his hat and handed it to me. That was one of the greatest acts of kindness I have ever known.

After the service, my mom and I went directly to Animal Control to get Rocco. When we approached his cage he was shivering and scared, but when he heard my voice, his tail wagged uncontrollably. I'm certain he thought I was Kelli.

32
THE BRACELET

After my family returned to Pennsylvania, I spent an excessive amount of time in bed, exhausted both physically and emotionally. I kept re-playing the conversation in my head from the way- back-when talk with Attorney Robert Haddad, "Because medical malpractice suits are so expensive to pursue most firms only take on cases that end in tragedies such as death or some sort of life-altering condition." But I had to hold it together as best I could for Brady. We would laugh and play until he tracked me down in the bathroom, sobbing. He was extremely compassionate and empathetic, wrapping his little arms around me in a moments' notice.

Creditors began calling my house phone within days of Kelli's death. I still don't know how they obtained my number, but somehow they did. And they were relentless, forcing me to scream into the phone to quit calling me. Several times they had asked for Kelli, which sent me over the edge. I felt like I was being stalked and harassed, feeling as though people thought that I was hiding Kelli at my house. It was unethical and distasteful on every level. Kelli didn't have any assets, so they were coming after me by default. She owned her condo but only for a year with little to no equity, which is why I had to let it go at a city auction.

I did have Kelli's black Ford Escape and couldn't bear to get rid of it. I know you loved it Kel. So even though mine was paid off and in great shape, I decided to refinance Kelli's and sell mine. But in order to refinance it, I had to wait thirty days before I could file for Executor of Estate, which meant that I had to hide Kelli's truck in my garage. For a month I wouldn't let anyone open that garage door, fearful that they'd confiscate the truck.

I asked my friend DeAngelo who is like another brother, to help move Kelli's belongings out of her condo. I wanted and needed to do that as quickly as possible for my own emotional well-being. And just as he always had in the past, he eagerly said yes and added, "I will even rent and drive the U-Haul to Kelli's place."

Me and Kelli were not Black Friday shoppers, but I did enjoy going to Home Depot to buy their 99-cent poinsettias. You could only buy ten and every year I would buy the max, keep nine, and take Kelli one. She thought I was crazy for getting up so early for plants, but I know that she enjoyed it.

So the Black Friday after her passing, I bought my plants and took one to her empty condo. I left it on the mantle over the fireplace. That was the only remaining item in her condo after I locked it up for the last time. The day after Thanksgiving within two months of starting to write this memoir, recollecting the memories, with shaking hands, I gently placed a poinsettia on the doorstep for whomever lives there now.

Her boxes sat in my garage for weeks before I could gather myself enough to go through them. Three of the boxes, three years later, still remain packed in the office at my home. Way too painful for me to move into the attic.

Kelli's best friend, Dana Miller, organized a memorial service at The Hershey Bar in Norfolk. Kelli and I spent countless Saturday nights there in our twenties dancing for hours. And we became friends with the owner, Annette Stone, who attended Kelli's funeral and kindly welcomed Dana's desire to honor my sister. Dana and I have become friends and I've grown to love and admire her, just as Kelli did. That night was truly special, meeting people that adored Kelli for her kindness and sense of humor. The bar was packed, a true accolade to my sister and the love that people had for her.

After Kelli's condo was completely emptied, I took Brady there to visit for the last time. He knew that his Aunt Kelli was in heaven by that point, but I wanted to give him an opportunity to visit before turning over the key. Kelli's condo had a great deck in the back that over-looked a small pond. She would sit out there, smoke her cigarettes, and feed the ducks. While we were visiting, a large cluster of ducks began swimming over to us as we stood outside, thrilling Brady. It ended up being such a nice moment, watching Brady kneel down peering through the deck's railings.

Kelli's Facebook account ended up turning into a memorial tribute, and although I was very grateful for the outpouring of love, I had it deactivated. It was just too painful. I also began reading her emails several times daily after figuring out her password. I would wait for the mailman eagerly each day, convinced that Kelli wrote me a letter, having someone else mail it. I did that for weeks, although I never received one. Everything that I did revolved around Kelli in one way or another. I'd drive to her condo several times weekly to check her mail. And if I couldn't get there, Maureen would go for me. On every envelope that came, I painfully scribbled 'deceased' and returned it to the mailbox. Often they were wet with tears and reluctant disbelief. Writing that word was sickening, even typing it now, sickens me.

A few weeks after Kelli's death, I was invited to lunch by Tom Pratt. Kelli often brought up his name during the last few weeks of her life. They got to know each other while Kelli was at the domiciliary; he was a peer group specialist. She had a great admiration for him, excited that he was helping her find a job. Tom also headed the Veteran X and Veteran Hope Programs, something I knew nothing about until meeting with him. He explained to me that Kelli felt strongly about needing a sister group to the Veteran X Program, suggesting Veteran Hope. She then assisted in developing the Veteran Hope's profile; a crucial piece of the program's beginning. When Tom and I first met, the exchange was filled with raw emotions and sadness. We vowed together to keep Kelli's name alive within the programs. Tom even created the Kelli Marie Grese Memorial Award that I've been fortunate to present three times. The award goes to an individual who goes above and beyond in their actions advocating for Vets in recovery. I present the award in the very same room that I visited Kelli in at the domiciliary. It's really hard to barricade my emotions from taking over. Sometimes I'm successful, other times not. But these Vets look forward to meeting Kelli's twin sister. Tom makes it a point to talk about Kelli often throughout the year, so by the completion of the program, they feel as though they know her. And when they see me, I become their tangible connection. They honor her by dressing in Steeler black and gold, they've put her name on their Christmas float for the holiday parade, and some tell stories of her kindness. And to me there's no greater tribute to my sister. Two years ago, I ordered some bracelets for the Vets; they're black and gold with an X and the message Never Lose Hope. And just two weeks ago, when I was I was going through a McDonald's drive thru, a gentleman opened the window to take my money. And as he reached out, I immediately noticed the bracelet on his wrist and a whirlwind of emotions took over. I choked a smile and whispered, "I'm Kelli's sister." He gasped, holding up his arm proudly as I slowly drove away. And in that moment, I knew that Kelli's death was not in vain. She's still touching lives daily just as she did when she was alive. I'm so proud of her and the legacy that's she left, hoping that one day I'll leave the same.

The programs Veteran X and Hope are helping Veterans to get their lives back, whether struggling with PTSD, addiction, mental illness etc. And hopefully they'll go national, throughout every Veterans Affairs Hospital and clinic nationwide. They've proven themselves successful and I'm committed to supporting Tom in his pursuit as Kelli's voice. To find out more, their website is http://veteran-x.webs.com/.

33
CASES THAT END IN TRAGEDY

Every day for the first month following Kelli's death, I'd read through her journal. Usually only being able to handle a couple of pages at a time. It was just too difficult. Kelli's entries were explicit and oppressive at times, but were also heartfelt and tender. And each time I read through her words, I still analyze and empathize, wishing I could have saved her. I find myself yearning for one last chance to make her feel safe as she did for me so many times throughout our lives together. But I failed. The years of chemicals proving much more powerful than me. The years of chemicals proving much more powerful-"only take on cases that end in tragedy"- my head was spinning.

When the day finally came where I could file for Executor of Estate I was panic stricken, finding it hard to catch my breath. Having to present Kelli's death certificate for any reason, paralyzed me each and every time. Her death still seemed inconceivable. Logically I knew what was happening, but emotionally I just couldn't connect with the reality that Kelli was gone.

I knew immediately after Kelli's death that I would

acquire Kelli's medical records from the Veterans Hospital to personally study what had transpired, in detail, over more than a decade of treatment. I vowed to continue fighting for Kelli against a system that I believed was responsible for her death. It was a system that proved to be extremely faulty and careless during the years of Kelli's treatment, at least in my lonely opinion.

I remember walking into the VA barely being able to swallow the lumps in my throat, fighting back the tears as hard as I could. I had to walk right in front of the two chairs that Kelli and I sat in while waiting for her to be taken to Salem, VA. It was re-living a nightmare. Everywhere I looked, I saw Kelli. I felt as though every Veteran and employee looking at me knew that I was immensely suffering, knew that I was fighting to not fall to pieces. After all, I was entering the facility that I felt was 100% responsible for my sister's death.

I took the elevator to the 2nd floor stuck in a mental trance. I approached the window, signed in with trembling fingers and waited for my name to be called. It seemed like it took forever. Still fighting back the tears, I pulled out my cell phone and began texting Kelli's number. I knew it was crazy, but I had to. I had to talk to her. *In a normal everyday way, I wanted to talk to you again.* I nervously approached, not knowing if I'd be given a hard time obtaining Kelli's records.

As the clerk pulled Kelli's name up in the system, I began having a full blown panic attack, something I would experience many times after this one. Panic has actually become a re-occurrence in my life since Kelli's death. Anyway, the lady was making every effort to be kind and explained that because Kelli's records were so vast, that it was going to take quite a while to print. She told me that she could mail them to me so I didn't have to wait. I graciously declined that offer, sat down, and waited.

It took well over an hour and the anticipation was agonizing. I just lived all of this, I knew what had happened, right? Did I? Trauma can confuse us in the moment. So getting the documented truth was terrifying. But I knew that I had to in order to pursue litigation. I had to prove without question, embellishment , and/or emotion that Kelli's death was in fact caused by years of over-medicating, and the only thing that could do that was Kelli's official records. When the printing was done, I was summoned to the window and handed two very large manila envelopes filled with thousands of pages. I had absolutely no idea how or where to begin.

When I got home that afternoon, my heart felt as though it was going to burst through my chest. I began thumbing through the records, a frustrating exercise that eventually became an obsession. I read and noted, I highlighted and screamed, and I cried and cursed. As I meticulously stepped through fourteen years of treatment, I labored through reliving emotions that were everywhere. I needed order. I began piecing everything together in a timeline format. There were times when my anxiety was paralyzing, but I pushed through it. I struggled to disconnect from the fact that I was reading through my twin sister's medical records. I had to trick my brain into thinking that I was reading someone else's history. Working at a trauma center helped me to do this. It's a survival technique that some medical professionals consider a must.

In between analyzing Kelli's records, I was also researching lawyers that specialized in Federal Tort Cases. Unfortunately, there were no local lawyers that did. So I put together a generalized letter, painting the most accurate picture that I could, and approached a few attorneys who were out of state via email. Two of them requested Kelli's records which meant that I had to have her records photocopied and mailed. So I rushed to Office Depot, copied the never-ending stacks and sent them off. I waited patiently, all along barely sleeping.

Balancing between motherhood and detective was tricky but Brady always took first position in the end, no matter what. Despite years of fighting alongside of Kelli,

I never faltered and fell apart. I had temporary melt downs, but I quickly gathered myself and carried on so I'd be damned if I was going to lose it now. I couldn't, Kelli still needed me and so did my little boy.

My gut told me that because of the size of Kelli's charts and the fact that I was located in a different state, neither law firm would take my case. So in the meantime, I went back to looking locally online. One night though, after Brady went to sleep, I had an epiphany. I needed to contact Robert Haddad. He didn't specialize in Federal Tort cases but he was the one who said, "Only take on cases that end in tragedy." He was also an extremely successful prosecutor. So I wrote him a long letter that night praying that he would contact me back. And the following day he did. He told me to gather Kelli's records and invited me to his office.

34
DARLA GRESE, PLAINTIFF
VS
THE UNITED STATES OF AMERICA, DEFENDANT

Entering the Shuttleworth, Ruloff, Swain, Haddad, and Morecock's law firm was at the very least, extremely intimidating. As my friend Maureen and I sat in the waiting room, I convinced myself that Bob would not take on my case. And in true, low self-esteem fashion, I self-sabotaged just as I always did. After feeling beat up for so many years, self-defeating thoughts were becoming the norm, or at least they became my norm.

When Bob appeared, he approached me with a soft smile on his face. He was very kind and at that moment, I felt as though I was in safe hands. He introduced himself to Maureen and took us into this spacious conference room. It had one of the largest tables that I'd ever seen. The décor was fancy, the surrounding book shelves beautiful, but somehow, sitting close to Bob, made the room feel quaint and small.

I placed the heavy box of records in front of me and began to talk nervously as he listened. Every once in a while Maureen would chime in as I missed a point, but I rambled on as Bob listened. I was crying my way through it, too, every so often having to stop to gather myself. I felt pathetic, broken, scared. I was so rattled by the notion that at the end of my rambling Bob would say that he couldn't help. He would say that he was sorry for my loss, but that he couldn't take my case. That is what I knew he would say.

When I finally finished, he excused himself for a few minutes while Maureen and I waited. I'm not sure that Maureen and I said two words to each other while we waited. Maureen was just as nervous for me. She knew the truth better than anyone. She witnessed it firsthand; the pills, Kelli's changes, she saw it all. She knew Kelli before Kelli began going to the VA. She saw the pills that were being delivered.

Bob returned with some paperwork. He told me that he was going to take Kelli's case. It was an emotional release, I spilled tears of hope. He felt strongly that if we considered only the last year of Kelli's life, the continued prescribing of the Seroquel, that would alone be enough. It was what he called a common-sense case. I couldn't believe that someone was going to help with the war that I had fought and constantly lost for so long.

I then had to muster the courage to ask him about payment. I was so afraid to ask that question. Was I going to have to sell my house? Kelli's car? Bob offered that if we go to trial and lose, I would only owe him $1000.00. I signed every piece of paper as quickly as I could. I thanked Bob multiple times through the weeping. He hugged me, offered me his condolences, and said he'd be in touch.

I left his office that day with mixed emotions. Hope had become a figment of my imagination after watching Kelli disappear. I wanted to celebrate, but I couldn't. Kelli was still dead and she was never coming back. But now I had someone fighting for her who was much more powerful than I ever was or could strive to become. I had an amazingly successful lawyer who was going to expose what the VA did in a way that I couldn't. Now I just had to wait, something that I wasn't good at doing.

After that meeting, my life became filled with depositions, copied correspondence, hearings, trial postponements, expert witnesses etc. I was officially engulfed in a world that I knew nothing about and it scared the hell out of me. I had never sued anyone for anything. Reading Darla Grese, Plaintiff VS The United States of America, Defendant on some of the correspondence was nauseating to say the least.

35
FIVE MILLION DOLLARS

On the day of my deposition I was a nervous wreck, having a stomach ache and cramping from stress. My fingers were almost numb from the anxiety and my voice unsteady. Bob prepped me the best he could, but I was still beside myself with fear. I knew that I was going to be grilled and raked over the coals with questions, but fortunately for me, all I had to do was tell the truth, which is exactly what I did. Bob, along with his assistant Carla, met with me beforehand and attempted to help with my emotions. I'm a little anxious to begin with so my anxiety throughout this thing was off the charts.

They escorted me into that same open conference room. This time though, there was nothing welcoming about it. There were two men dressed in fancy suits, sternly sitting at the table quietly waiting for me. A court reporter flanked them. I wish I could say that they were nice and welcoming, but cold-as-ice is a much more accurate description. They were stone-faced cold. Still though, I greeted them kindly because I know no other way. Kelli knew no other way. And this was for Kelli and those after her.

For three hours, I was questioned. They asked questions that I hadn't dreamed they would ask. By the end of it, I felt emotionally raped. I had nothing left… nothing. My head was throbbing, my heart longed for Kelli, and my brain was mush. Even Bob was surprised at how long the deposition had lasted. He and Carla knew that I was depleted.

And then came the settlement hearings. Although I'm not permitted to discuss those in detail, I will say this…I felt like a vulnerable little girl when I walked into those rooms. There was a judge, two stone-faced expensive suits, Bob, and me. There were words thrown around that I couldn't pronounce let alone know the meaning of. The only thing I did know is that I didn't want to settle. I would leave those hearings, go to my car, and cry, having to gather myself before even starting the ignition. Those hearings were painful in more ways than I ever care to recount.

For months, I would eagerly wait for the mail to arrive. I breathed , ate, and slept the lawsuit. Once the media caught wind of the lawsuit and the local newspaper interviewed me, I was stunned when the headline included the dollar amount that we were suing for. Five million dollars. I had absolutely nothing to do with choosing that figure. As a matter of fact, I didn't even know what it was until I got the official letter from Bob's office. I was thinking, "People will automatically assume that I am in this for the money." And I was right, some did, which was like stabbing my soul with chards of glass. For so many years I fought this battle for Kelli, for a viable future for those in situations like Kelli, without asking anyone for anything. And now. Now people were placing judgment on me?

I had to forge on. Kelli had gone through too much for it to be in vain. And she is not the only one. Since her death, others continue to suffer in a system that does not accommodate long term in-house care for substance abuse & mental illness. The day before twenty-four year old Austin (Gus) Deeds stabbed his father (a Virginia State Senator) and then killed himself,

Gus was released by a mental health facility that said there were no more psychiatric beds available.

Could the money have changed my life and my family's? Absolutely. Do I believe that the VA deserved to be sued for the maximum amount possible? Absolutely. Could any dollar amount replace the loss that I've suffered? That we have suffered, those that knew Kelli, and those that are finding out who she was right now in this memoir? No. I wanted my day in court. I had been robbed of the simple life that I once knew with my sister, my best friend. My Kelli was gone and they took her from me. That is how I felt. That is how I still feel.

36
DO YOU HEAR ME NOW?

Once Bob agreed to take the case, I still struggled with letting go. I had absolutely no clue on how to stop fighting, because I had done it for so long. I knew that no matter what, at the end of the day, nobody could know Kelli's struggle better than me. No one could prove this case better than I could. I fought in the trenches with Kelli. So I began dissecting Kelli's chart, word for word, pill by pill. I bought a red plastic box that I could keep her records in. I purchased folders that I could separate parts of the chart with. I had a system and every morning, usually at 4 AM or earlier, I would pull out my red plastic box and get to work. And when I had to work at the hospital, I took papers with me. I always had something with me that I could read and study. Somehow, I felt like I had too. And all along, very few people even knew what I was in the midst of. I've always been an extremely private person as was Kelli, so I kept a small circle of friends who I confided in, I still do to this day.

I essentially put together a timeline of the VA's treatment of Kelli. And this process ended up becoming one of the most painful experiences of my life. It haunted me, infuriating me even more.

I designed a spreadsheet and named it Partial Med List. It listed some of the most powerful medications that were dispensed to Kelli. I listed the pill's name and how many pills were dispensed to Kelli each year. It spanned from 1998 through 2010. I actually kept re-counting the numbers because I was certain that the quantities couldn't be correct. I even had a friend count as well to insure that I wasn't somehow delusional, seeing numbers that weren't actually there. I wasn't though, the numbers were disturbingly correct.

I then began typing out what I titled "Darla's Review." I merely pulled out significant doctor notes, inconsistencies, pills quantities etc. Anything that I deemed relevant, I incorporated. It was after a "defense expert review" of Kelli's chart that I began this obsession. His review enraged me, my blood boiled. I couldn't believe that this medical professional could exaggerate and conveniently leave out pertinent information. He skillfully marched through Kelli's chart with a sarcastic and arrogant manor. He was painting an inaccurate and unfair picture of Kelli. How dare he make my sister appear to be something that she wasn't? It was war. I had been at it for a long time. Now, the anger, moved me to fight even more.

I spent several weeks rebutting everything that he had said during his embellished review. Kelli was being portrayed as a desperate, drug-seeking, pot-smoking woman, instead of a female Veteran who fell victim to the grips of addiction, which in turn, led to chemically-induced psychosis. She was a human being that became addicted to the pills that they continued to supply her. She had a disease. Do you hear me now? Can you add this to your notes?

The synopsis I titled "Darla's Review" is long, very long. But I hope you will read it in its entirety. Grammatically its' mediocre at best. At the end of the day, it was only meant for Bob and his team to read. But in order to tell Kelli's complete story, I have to share it in this book.

37
DRUGS, DRUGS, AND MORE DRUGS
Darla's Review (# = number of pills)

Dr. Expert states that Kelli was prescribed sleeping medication while still on active duty. I believe it's important to point out that these medications were prescribed only for a brief amount of time, 2-3 weeks to be specific. (page 1331 As I've stated previously, Kelli was extremely successful during her entire Navy Career, including the last 2 years, post break-in. Her evaluations were superb; she was nominated for Junior Sailor of the Quarter at the end of her career, managed and participated on the command color guard team, scored outstanding on her physical readiness test etc…

Dr. Expert mentions that Kelli was seen in March and prescribed the benzodiazepine Ativan 3 mg at bedtime (significant dose), but what he failed to mention was that the VA was also prescribing Kelli Clonazapam, per the Rx Profile (page 9), another addictive benzo at the very same time in significant dosages. Examples are as follows… #450 on 3/19/98, #60 on 7/24/98, #60 on 10/15/98, #60 on 11/9/98 and #60 on 11/19/98. On 11/19/98, #30 Lorazapam were prescribed in addition to the #60 Clonazapam. This is how Kelli's addiction to benzos transpired which lead her to the first admission on 3/15/99. Dr. Expert states that Kelli was seen again in June and was experiencing "similar" symptoms as she did from the break-in. However, after reading the package insert for Clonazapam, I was stunned to read that nearly every symptom that Kelli was experiencing, including the worsening depression, irritability, weight loss, and anxiety was/is listed under "Possible Adverse Reactions."

Kelli then sees Dr. --- (resident) on June 2, 1998. (Page 1332) The doctor "discusses" the risk of benzo dependence. But somehow, in 1998 alone, by my count on the Rx profile, #750 Clonazapam were prescribed in addition to #450 Ativan, both extremely addictive benzodiazepines. Dr. --- then prescribes Serzone, another sedating drug, but Kelli complains of worsening insomnia and headaches, ironically, these are two symptoms listed under possible adverse reactions of Clonazapam, which apparently no one has picked up on yet. The Neurontin, another very sedating drug is prescribed. **I'm not sure at this point how anyone could be surprised that Kelli's missing scheduled appointment's due to the amount of sedating meds that's she's on.**

Dr. Expert states that Klonopin (Clonazapam) was then prescribed on 7/24/98. He states this, in my opinion, confusingly, as if this is the 1st time that this medicine was prescribed. But in fact, as mentioned above, and per the Rx profile, Clonazapam was actually started on 3/19/98 with #450 pills.

Dr. --- states that Kelli's benefiting from the benzos, although in relatively larger doses. However, in his note, (page 1327) he states that Kelli feels depressed, loss of pleasurable activities, frequent crying spells, sleeplessness and flashbacks. Again, most of these are listed under possible adverse reactions on the package insert to Clonazapam. So I'm not sure how she's really benefiting from benzos? She's simply addicted to them. In my opinion, she does not "tolerate" anti-depressants simply because they do not give her the sedating "escape" that the benzos provide. Dr. --- then states that she seems to not be abusing her meds. Then why in just 1998 alone, has she been prescribed #450 Lorazapam and #750 Clonazapam per the Rx profile?

Dr. Expert states that Kelli then begins to cancel appointments. In my opinion, this is because she's now addicted to the benzos and can hardly hold her head up let alone drive. Again, on the package insert to Clonazapam, it warns patients to avoid driving while taking this medication. She also complained of abdominal pain, which again, in the package insert to Clonazapam, is listed under possible adverse reactions. Dr. Expert also mentions that Kelli was being prescribed Vicodin. The Hampton VA was prescribing her Percocet, Tylenol with Codeine, and Demerol in quite impressive quantities. These are listed on page 6 of the Rx profile.

On 3/16/99, Kelli was admitted to the inpatient psychiatric unit for detox. Kelli was addicted to the medications that the VA was prescribing, specifically, the benzodiazepines, that included the Ativan and Clonazapam.

Dr. Expert points out that Kelli stated that she's been unemployed for a year and is having many "up and down" moods, lack of motivation and isolation and decreased activity. In my opinion, this is because the VA was prescribing an enormous amount of "downers", which benzos are, which made it impossible for Kelli to function at this point. **By my count per the Rx profile, in 1999 alone, 5,370 Clonazapam were prescribed. Somehow this is/was legal?**

Dr. Expert states that Kelli saw Dr. --- on 3/25/99 and that he recommended Kelli cut back on her meds. She then sees him again on 4/8/99 and apparently he thought that although she had experienced some worsening anxiety, she was tolerating the taper so far. Kelli returns on 4/22/99 and says that's she's "succeeding" in the taper. So she's then prescribed another #450 Clonazapam, the exact same drug that she was admitted for on her first admission because she was addicted to it.

I think it's obvious that she was still addicted to the drug at this point. On 5/21 (page 1312), she complains of feeling terrible, irritable, depressed, with repeated migraines. Again, all listed in the Clonazapam insert as possible adverse reactions.

Once again Kelli is transferred to another resident, Dr. ---. Kelli mentioned that she feared reduction of Klonopin would worsen her anxiety, so Dr. --- kept it as is, regardless of Kelli's history of being addicted to this specific drug. Kelli apparently cancels some appointments. Perhaps it's because she received #450 Clonazapam on 4/22/99, #450 on 5/7/99, #450 on 6/4/99, #450 on 7/6/99, #450 on 8/13/99, #450 on 10/1/99, #450 on 10/7/99, 10/26/99, #450 on 11/5/99 and the list continues. I'm guessing Kelli was sleeping during her scheduled appointments that she missed.

During an evaluation on 9/9/99, Kelli reported palpitations, nightmares, shakes, muscle cramps, shortness of breath (dyspnea), and stomach aches etc... which again, according to the package insert to Clonazapam, are possible adverse reactions. It's mentioned that Clonazapam has been tapered off recently. But per the Rx profile, #450 Clonazapam were dispensed on 8/13/99.

On 10/1/99, Kelli met with Dr. --- and apparently Kelli was very irritable about her condition and frustrated. Again, according to the package insert for Clonazapam, irritability, aggressive behavior and agitation are very possible on this drug. At this point, Kelli has presented with countless side effects that could have been directly related to the extremely high dosages of Clonazapam, but not one physician has mentioned this or even picked up on it.

It's noted then that Kelli couldn't remember if she'd been on Serzone before so it again was re-started. However, if Dr. --- would have looked further back in the records, he would have seen that Kelli was in fact on

Serzone in the past and Kelli said that it caused insomnia and headaches.

Then Doxepin, another sedating drug, was prescribed and the Clonazapam was increased by Dr. ---. I'd like to point out that in the package insert for Clonazapam; it states that the physician who elects to use Klonopin for extended periods should periodically reevaluate the long-term usefulness of the drug. **On page 3 it states that the effectiveness of Klonopin in long term use, that is more than 9 weeks, has NOT been systematically studied in controlled clinical trials.**

Kelli again presents herself angrily on 11/6/99, a potential adverse reaction from the Clonazapam. When Kelli first began seeing the VA, she was not angry, she was never unkind and would certainly have never yelled at a physician, yet again, it's never discussed that the Clonazapam, in addition to all of the other meds, were making this person essentially angry, addicted and hopeless. Instead, she was diagnosed with Personality Disorder with Borderline Features. They "asked" her to cut back on her Klonopin instead of just limiting the means of her getting it in incredibly high numbers. On the very day she sees Dr. ---, on 12/9/99, #450 more Clonazapam were dispensed.

In early 2000, Kelli began to increasingly complain of headaches. In the Clonazapam package insert, headaches are listed under possible adverse reactions. Although Kelli already had a history of migraine headaches documented, the fact that they were worsening should have perhaps raised a red flag. And at this point, Kelli was on incredibly large amounts of Clonazapam. Per the Rx profile, in 1999, Kelli was prescribed 5,370 Clonazapam.

On page 1275 in Kelli's chart, Dr. --- writes on June 27, 2000...

"Would avoid narcotics if possible for the treatment of chronic pain. I also note a history of benzodiazepine dependency in the past and would use these medications with care."

In 2000, the VA was prescribing Percocet, Demerol and Tylenol with Codeine. In 2000, per the Rx profile, #320 Percocet, #360 Tylenol with Codeine and #240 Demerol were dispensed to Kelli.

I ended up having to sell our house that we owned together in July 2000 simply because I couldn't watch her slowly kill herself any longer. It got to the point where I was anxious when I would see the mailman pull up because I knew what he was bringing. We loved our home and it was devastating to let it go and for the first time ever, live separate from one another.

It's noted that Kelli is getting meds from an outside doctor, Dr. ---. Kelli stated that she was getting Elavil and Percocet from him. If this was the case, I'm wondering why the VA would continue to prescribe narcotics to Kelli if in fact, per their note, she was apparently getting narcotics from Dr. ---. The VA continued to prescribe Percocet, Tylenol with Codeine and Demerol. And since they knew the doctor's name, couldn't they have called Dr. --- to discuss the details of Kelli's medications and what she was being prescribed, especially a patient with Kelli's history? Or did they simply not care?

On 4/4/00, a nurse even makes note of Kelli's meds and the frequency of her refills. This is on page 1303 of Kelli's chart

Dr. --- sees Kelli on 4/7/00, she complains of increased nightmares, which again, in the package insert for Clonazapam, is listed under possible adverse reactions. She states that she's "interested" in Valium in place of Clonazapam. He notes that she hasn't abused Clonazapam in several months. However, I'm not sure what he based that on since the VA had just dispensed #450 on 3/10/00 and #450 on 3/30/00! And then #450 more on 4/13/00 which is after their meeting. So apparently the Clonazapam that was supposed to "be replaced" by the Valium, was still being prescribed in addition to the #120 Valium that were dispensed on 4/7/00. In fact, per the Rx profile, the Clonazapam wasn't stopped until 2002.

On 4/10/00, (page 1300) Dr. --- notes "will taper and stop the Valium". This never happened. In fact, per the Rx profile, in 2000, Kelli was dispensed #1080, and in 2001, #1200.

Dr. --- states that Dr. --- discontinued the Valium and switched back to the Klonopin. However, per the Rx profile, that absolutely never happened.

Kelli sees Dr. --- on 5/15/00 (page 1299) and complains of ongoing anxiety, back spasms and migraines. Again, in the package insert for Klonopin, back pains, anxiety and migraines are listed. Kelli also requested to switch back from Klonopin to Valium, which Dr. --- notes that he did. However, according to the Rx profile, he did not. Instead, both drugs were given.

Dr. --- notes that Kelli complained of back, shoulder and neck pain. Again, these are listed under possible adverse reactions of Klonopin.

On page 1287 of Kelli's chart, she admitted to Dr. ---, that she needed to take extremely high doses of both her Valium and Klonopin to obtain relief of panic attacks. Their phone call was on 6/8/00. Kelli agreed to return unused Valium (23 tabs) and Klonopin (31 tabs) the following day and then he'll write for a new prescription of Valium and Klonopin in different dosages. What's alarming though, in addition to what Kelli was being prescribed, is the fact that Kelli only had 31 tablets of Klonopin left after having been dispensed #450 on 5/5/00. Dr. --- never questions this. Instead, the following day, the pharmacy dispenses #60 more and #120 Valium.

Kelli is complaining of severe neck and shoulder pain. She ends up actually being admitted for it. However, all her films turn up negative. In the package insert for Klonopin, nape pain (neck pain) and shoulder pain are again, listed under possible adverse reactions. It's obvious at this point to me that Kelli's addicted to her meds and she's suffering tremendously from the side effects of being on such a large amount for so long now. The internal medicine team even mentioned that they were concerned about Kelli being over-medicated, particularly with narcotics, and that they should be tapered off. On page 1279 of Kelli's chart, Dr. --- writes that he voiced his medical concern to Kelli in regards to analgesic med related side effects and the cost benefit ratio. Still, the VA continued to prescribe per the Rx profile on page 6, Demerol, Percocet and Tylenol with Codeine, even after Kelli's hospitalization.

Kelli ends up leaving the hospital AMA.

(Page 1261) On 7/31/00 Kelli is seen by Dr. --- who actually recommends to Kelli an admission to their inpatient psych unit to get off of the high dose benzos, but Kelli declines. Dr. --- even states that it's her impression, r/o adverse cognitive effects due to medications.

Unfortunately, the medications were continued, including both the benzos and narcotics.

(Pages1260/1261) On 9/21/00, after a team meeting was ordered by the chief of staff, Dr. --- states that he will stop prescribing both valium and Klonopin together, since valium is in fact not indicated for muscle spasms. However, that did not happen. #120 Valium were dispensed on 10/20/00 and #60 Klonopin on 10/3/00.

What's not noted in the chart is the reason this meeting was called by the Chief of Staff. I uninvitingly and desperately went into his office and made a plea for him to stop his staff from writing these prescriptions that were destroying my sister. This was one of the many pleas that I made.

(Page 1243) On 10/19/00, it's noted that Kelli's an agitated, tense, and unhappy women experiencing numerous physical problems. It's sad to read this note because everything that Kelli was displaying over these prior months are listed under the possible adverse reactions of Klonopin, the very drug that she was receiving in huge quantities. This includes agitation, aggressiveness, depression, aches, pains, headaches, hostility etc… but instead of weaning

Kelli off of this drug, they instead diagnose her with Somatoform Disorder, Passive-aggressive traits etc…

It goes on to say…caretakers are soon put off by her nonspecific description of symptoms, apparent noncompliance with treatment recommendations, and seemingly continual complaints of new ailments. This note also angers me… not one single doctor yet has even mentioned the possibility of all these new "ailments" being caused by the Clonazapam and that these "aliments" to Kelli were extremely real.

(Page 1238) Kelli called complaining of severe knee pain. Again, Klonopin insert for possible adverse reactions.

She sees Dr. --- on 11/16/00, and not surprisingly, he increases her Klonopin to 6 mg per day and states that he's going to d/c the valium. However, Kelli receives #120 Valium on 1/9/00 and 1/26/00.

(Page 1222) Kelli sees Dr. ---, she complains of severe back pain. She appeared very anxious and depressed. Again, back pain is listed as a possible adverse reaction to Klonopin in addition to increased anxiety and depression. He also mentioned that she was angry during most of her session, another documented possible side effect of the drug.

(Page 1214) Kelli presents to Dr. --- on 1/8/01 with severe left foot pain and numbness. Again, Klonopin package insert lists foot pain as possible adverse reaction. **She states that it "feels as though someone is holding a cigarette lighter to my foot." Burning skin is also listed as a possible adverse reaction to Klonopin.**

He then refills her Valium for 5 months for muscle spasms. It appears that almost every time Kelli asks for a medication, she receives it, regardless of the fact that she's obviously experiencing severe side effects and is in fact addicted.

(Page 1205) Kelli's then seen on 3/12/00 in Neurology, she was volatile and easily angered. Again, listed in the package insert of Klonopin as a possible adverse reaction. She ended up leaving the appointment angry before even seeing Dr. ---.

(Page 1195/1196) Kelli presented to the ER with a small shard of glass in her right thumb. It's noted that the laceration is too small to suture. Still, they prescribed her #40 Percocet.

(Page 1184) Kelli sees Dr. --- on 8/10/01. Kelli states that she's moved to Virginia Beach and that the move was stressful. Dr. --- agrees to CONTINUE both the valium and Clonazapam (Klonopin) and to also increase the Doxepin. He states that "she hasn't abused these meds lately." Although, I'm not sure what he bases that on since she's still taking significantly high doses of these drugs.

Dr. --- speaks of Kelli's first of many admissions to Virginia Beach Psychiatric Center that occurred on 9/1/01. Not surprisingly, it was noted that Kelli had a history of abusing Demerol, Percocet and Clonazapam.

It was noted that Kelli was angry, out of control and had slurred speech. These are all possible adverse reactions to Clonazapam as I've stated numerous times elsewhere.

Kelli then is transferred to Salem, Virginia on 9/5/01 which was most likely due to Hampton not having enough beds for women, something that was a frequent problem. Salem changed her diagnosis to Polysubstance Dependence.

Salem VA notes that Kelli had a history of cancelling appointments, frequent complaints of pain that failed to show pathology, frequently becoming agitated etc… again, these are all possible adverse reactions to Clonazapam. Not to mention being on several other meds such as valium, narcotics, barbiturates, tricyclic antidepressants etc…

It's also noted that my family and I voiced concern that Kelli was receiving bags of pills in the mail from the VA and that Kelli had significant substance abuse problems. It was also noted that I said that Kelli was getting pills from other "personal sources." I told them that many times over the years in hopes that they would stop

dispensing so many drugs to her. If I thought that telling them Jesus himself was sending her pills would get them to stop, then I would have told them that as well.

(Page 1181) Kelli sees Dr. --- on 11/2/01 accompanied by myself. It's noted that she was in great spirits and "doing well." Salem stopped all meds with the exception of two anti-depressants Celexa and Trazodone. She was no longer angry, irritable, demanding etc…

(Page 1180) Kelli sees Dr. --- on 3/14/02 and not surprisingly, Kelli's still doing very well. He notes that she's pleasant, cooperative, alert with good eye contact.

(Page 1171) Kelli sees Dr. ---. She states that she's doing well. She's going to college, has no problems with sleep, denies depression or manic symptoms, has no problems with appetite is staying clean and sober. She says "sometimes has some anxiety."

(Page 1166) Kelli sees Dr. --- on 9/17/02. Again, she's pleasant, cooperative, alert, continues in college and is doing well. **She only complains of having anxiety "sometimes". Dr. --- begins a "trial of Seroquel 25 mg for anxiety and sleep."**

(Page 1158) On 11/18/02, Kelli tells Dr. --- in regards to the Seroquel "sometimes it helps and sometimes it doesn't."

(Page 1148) Kelli sees Dr. --- on 12/19/02. Kelli states that she was doing well until a few days ago when she began having trouble sleeping. She's still in college, pleasant, cooperative and she says she's staying clean and sober.

Dr. --- decided to **increase her "trial" of Seroquel to 100-200 mg for sleep and anxiety in addition to prescribing valium, one of the benzodiazepines that Kelli was addicted too in the past!**

Kelli was a recovering prescription drug addict and instead of Dr. --- realizing that Kelli was possibly on her way to a relapse, he instead, prescribes more meds.

It's noted that Kelli canceled many appointments at the VA. But when she did speak with Dr. --- on

1/28/04, she told him that she was doing well in college. I wanted to make note that this is several times already in the chart that Kelli made reference to how well she did with her studies. **She never complained about suffering from ADHD or difficulty concentrating.**

On 5/6/04, Kelli informs Dr. --- that she's stopped taking the Seroquel due to its sedating effects. Per the Rx profile, the last prescription that Kelli filled was on 8/26/03. Dr. --- notes that Kelli's well kept, pleasant, cooperative, good eye contact etc… She also states that she's doing well at Tidewater Community College.

This notes the 1st documented psychotic break for Kelli. She was admitted to VA Beach Psych on 1/5/05. Kelli states that she's been seeing Dr. --- for ADHD and takes Adderall. Her drug screen was negative for cannabis, but Dr. Expert "questions" the reliability of the test since most subsequent tests were positive for cannabis. However, I've found since reviewing the records, that the admissions into Virginia Beach psych on 9/1/01 4/25/05, and 5/2/05, and were also negative.

Kelli enters voluntarily the VBPC's outpatient Treatment Program. She reports to Dr. --- that she feels really depressed with mood swings. Dr. Expert points out that Kelli at one point says she's getting her meds from her primary care physician and yet at another time, she makes no reference to having one. After years of going through Kelli's meds, the VA was in fact where she was getting her meds, which is also evident by her Rx Profile. She certainly could have gotten Adderall from Dr. ---, but since we cannot view his records, we simply do not know. Kelli considered her PCP her MD at the VA, whomever that was at the time, which changed quite often as the records show. Also, throughout Dr. Expert's review, he makes note of Kelli's inconsistencies as far as meds, dosages etc… but at this point and after all of these years of taking such high quantities, I'm not sure how this could even be surprising.

Kelli again addresses her depression, which unfortunately in my opinion, was never appropriately treated to begin with. Instead, anti-psychotics, anti-convulsants, narcotics, stimulants, anti-manics, sedatives, benzodiazepines and barbiturates were prescribed instead. What Kelli needed was a consistent psychotherapist, not psychiatrist. Dr. Expert also reports "strikingly" that Kelli reports to having smoked marijuana daily for the past 15 years, but obvious by her records, this is incorrect and again reflects her just telling them what she presumed they wanted to hear. Kelli also thought the CIA was after her, but I'm certain they didn't take her word on that, so why would they believe she smoked pot every day for 15 years even after testing negatively upon several admissions? Also, we got out of the Navy in 1997, so if Kelli smoked pot for 15 years, we would have been active duty for some of that. We were tested every couple of months while active duty, so obviously Kelli wasn't smoking pot!

Dr. Expert states that Dr. --- during that admission (2/22/05 – 3/28/05) "somewhat surprisingly" made some medication changes right at the start of the admission and stopped her Seroquel and Celexa, and started Topamax, Neurontin, Zoloft and Geodon. But looking at the Rx Profile, on page 14, **Seroquel was never discontinued**. Also, the first Neurontin wasn't dispensed until 8/11/10 per page 10 on the Rx Profile. Also, on page 12 of the Rx Profile, you'll see that Celexa was actually stopped on 8/26/03 before finally being started again on 4/18/06. So point being, Dr. --- "surprising" changes were actually quite minimal according to Kelli's records.

Kelli was re-admitted to Virginia Beach Psych on 4/25/05 for depression. Her urine drug screen was negative for cannabis, although this surprises Dr. Expert. Kelli then went back to their partial hospitalization program from 5/2/05-5/27/05. **She presented with worsening anxiety in the context of using marijuana (2+ joints every night). But**

according to the discharge summary of this specific admission, the lab findings were unremarkable. However, it's never noted anywhere to my knowledge that any physician asks Kelli why she says she smokes pot constantly when in fact, proven by lab findings, she did not. Was she being dishonest for some reason or did she in fact believe that she was smoking it every night?

I'd like to also point out that per the VA medical records, Kelli had negative cannabis results on pages 60, 67, 68, 69, 155, 166, 168 and 247.

Dr. Expert again lists all of the med changes that Dr. --- makes. He also states that Dr. --- prescribed a tricyclic antidepressant and notes that these medicines are generally considered to be psychotropic which are most likely to exacerbate cycling or induce mania in bipolar disorder. On page 11 of the Rx Profile, 3 tricyclic medicines were given by the VA in Kelli's earlier years. Also, Dr. Expert states that "confusingly" the discharge sheet from VBPC only lists Zoloft, Seroquel and Lithium. However, that's incorrect. The discharge summary lists in addition to Zoloft, Seroquel and Lithium, Buspar, and Imipramine.

Dr. Expert mentions that Dr. --- "raised" the issue of possible ADHD, although did not prescribe Adderall. I think it's important to point out that on the discharge summary of this admission, there's no mention of ADHD or even r/o ADHD. The discharge diagnoses were Major depression, r/o Bipolar, PTSD and r/o Borderline Personality Disorder.

This is part of Dr. --- ADHD "screening." He concludes that Kelli's depression and anxiety have probably added some degree of forgetfulness and poor concentration. He "suspects" the she has had an attention deficit hyperactivity disorder, inattentive type. To my knowledge, his conclusions are solely based on Kelli's answers to basic questions and not by a phone call to the VA perhaps questioning Kelli's doctors who know her history well in addition to her prescription drug abuse history, including psychosis.

Dr. --- sees Kelli on 5/16/05 (page 1108/1109) and Kelli explains that Dr. --- diagnoses her with Bipolar and ADD. Kelli states that she a history of poor concentration, although from what I've read in the charts, Kelli never reported this to Dr. --- or anyone at the VA until now. Actually, she's reported only to the contrary, that's she's done very well in college, Navy etc... However, instead of questioning this or confirming this with Dr. ---, he instead prescribes Dexadrine, since the VA didn't carry Adderall. He does this knowing that Kelli has a prescription for Strattera. Dexadrine is an amphetamine which clearly warns patients of its highly addictive traits and potential long lists of possible complications, including increased depression, psychosis etc…

(Page 1102) Kelli spoke with Dr. --- on the phone after canceling her appointments with him. He refilled her Seroquel, Phenobarbital and Zoloft, on 8/19/05. Given Kelli's history, calling in a controlled substance like Phenobarbital I would think would require physically seeing the person rather than just speaking to them over the phone.

Dr. Expert notes that Kelli has a seizure less than 24 hours after discharge from VBPC and that it "could have been" from an abrupt discontinuation from Phenobarbital. I think this is a ridiculous statement. First and foremost, according to the records from Kelli's stay at VBPC, there's no mention what so ever that Kelli was even taking Phenobarbital during her stay and the discharge meds were only listed as Seroquel and Zoloft. I can't imagine that the physicians at VBPC would keep Kelli on Phenobarbital during her 4 day stay and then send her home, abruptly stopping it. **I was there during Kelli's seizure and it occurred almost immediately upon her taking the Seroquel.**

(Page 1084/1085) Kelli sees Dr. --- again on 4/18/06. She states that she's still feeling anxious. She also states that the daytime Seroquel makes her very tired. So Dr. --- again prescribes the very addicting barbiturate Phenobarbital, which too, according to the insert, is a sedative. Given Kelli's history of canceling her appointments and documented seizure, I'm not sure why Dr. --- would choose to prescribe Phenobarbital being that it's supposed to be monitored extremely closely due to its risk of seizures if stopped abruptly and its addictive potential.

(Page 1073/1074) Kelli then sees Dr. --- again on 5/23/06 and she states that "she is feeling better." Dr. --- then begins prescribing the anticonvulsant Topamax, which comes with its own list of precautions/warnings listed below from package insert. I find it interesting that he chose a medication that lists under frequent reactions, hallucinations and psychosis given Kelli's history. Also, Topamax can increase the occurrence of migraines, which obviously Kelli complains of consistently.

(Page 1073/1074) Kelli sees Dr. --- on 8/14/06. She's having nightmares and has anxiety due to bankruptcy court. Instead of perhaps explaining that being anxious about this is a normal, human response, he instead adds Geodon, another antipsychotic, in addition to the Topamax and Seroquel.

(Page 1071/1072) Kelli sees Dr. --- again on 10/30/06 and she tells him that she felt "paranoid" on the Geodon and stopped it after one dose. She also stated that the Topamax made her more anxious so she stopped it and then felt less anxious. She also hasn't been taking the Seroquel during the day still because of the sedating effects of it.

Dr. Expert states that Dr. --- "lowers" Kelli's Seroquel, but it was actually Kelli who stopped taking the daytime Seroquel by her own choice. Dr. --- simply states 150-200 mg at night. Dr. Expert states that Kelli had required larger doses of Seroquel when acutely psychotic, however, I dispute this statement. **When Kelli was admitted to VBPC, Kelli was always placed on several medications in addition to Seroquel. So I don't believe anyone can say that the Seroquel in higher doses was effective or ineffective. In most of 2003 and all of 2004, Kelli**

was completely off of Seroquel, in addition to most of the other potent meds that the VA prescribed over the years and she had zero episodes of psychosis.

If you look at the chart of meds I designed, pay attention to the years 2002-2004. These were the years that the VA backed off on meds. Kelli had no hospitalizations during these three years. In 2005, she was hospitalized at least five times and obvious by the chart, the meds began coming again.

(Pages 1004, 1005, 1006) I think it's important to mention here that on 8/21/07, Kelli sees Dr. --- and during her interview she states that Kelli's concentration is good, without any mention of ADHD symptoms of any sort. Kelli was well-groomed, cooperative and her "memory and calculation are grossly intact."

Dr. Expert does not mention that prior to Kelli seeing Dr. --- on 9/19/07, on 9/12/07; Kelli was prescribed #120 Tylenol with Codeine and a Codeine expectorant according to pages 6 and 21 of the Rx Profile.

(Pages 994-997) Kelli sees Dr. --- and states that her mood has not changed since the last visit. She states that some symptoms have improved although the anxiety and panic attacks "have not subsided as much as she would have liked." So instead of perhaps discussing ways of developing and learning better coping skills, instead, an anti-anxiety medication is added to the mix. Buspar is added three times a day.

(Pages 925-928) Kelli sees Dr. --- on 3/7/08. Again, just another copy and paste of the chief complaint.

(Pages 920-924) Kelli sees Dr. --- on 4/11/08. Chief complaint is again copied and pasted.

Kelli's admission to Ms. --- in regards to being a "stoner," in my personal opinion, and having known Kelli better than anyone, was a simple symptom of how she saw and felt about herself. She had terrible self-esteem and saw herself as a loser by this point. Again, as I've said previously, throughout the years, Kelli's drug screens were frequently negative for marijuana, which concludes that her use of the drug was occasional at best. Matter of fact, Kelli told me that she would smoke an occasional joint to off-set the effects of the meds that made her feel anxious.

(Pages 904-907) Kelli sees Dr. --- on 6/7/08. Chief complaint's identical to previous ones. It's noted that Kelli states she got Ativan from her pcp and feels terrible about it. **It's important to note, this Ativan was dispensed by the VA on 4/18/08 and 5/8/08 per the Rx Profile on page 8. Ativan is a benzodiazepine, the drug that Kelli was 1st addicted too.**

(Pages 901-904) Kelli sees Dr. ---, another resident on 7/7/08. Tragically, he begins her on the very same benzo that nearly destroyed Kelli years earlier, Clonazapam. And of course the chief complaint is a mirror image of previous ones.

Dr. Expert also notes that on 9/26/08, Dr. --- placed a non-formulary request to the pharmacy for Adderall. I'm unable to locate these pages in the chart so I'm not able to give you the page numbers. Kelli apparently told him that she "benefited" from Ritalin in the past. In my opinion, Kelli at this point has relapsed, she's back on benzos and the physicians following her continue to alternate, without proper review of Kelli's history and past hospitalizations.

Kelli sees him again on 12/1/08. He then increases the Seroquel and adds Ritalin to the mix. On 12/1/08, #60 Ritalin were dispensed in addition to #60 N/F Amphetamine/Dextroamph Resin 20 mg, which I believe is a generic form of Adderall, but not positive. Both are extremely addictive stimulants. So on this one day alone, she received #120 pills (stimulants).

Not surprisingly, Kelli was admitted to VBPC on 3/15/09 for psychosis, paranoia of the CIA following her etc. her lab findings were unremarkable.

Dr. Expert suggests that the dosages were not very high. I think it's important to note that on 2/20/09, #120 stimulants were again dispensed to Kelli. This is on page 16 of the Rx Profile.

In my opinion, perhaps this isn't considered "high" to the average person who actually suffers from ADHD, but to a recovering drug addict with a documented history of abusing amphetamines, it is.

There's even a note in Kelli's chart on page 858, 5/29/09, noting in all caps.. **"HAVE DISCONTINUED MEDS DUE TO LIKELY CONTRIBUTION TO HER SUDDEN MOOD CHANGES. DO NOT RETURN TO STIMLUANT MEDICATIONS!**

Shockingly, on 12/4/09, #60 stimulants were again dispensed to Kelli. This is shown on page 16 of Rx Profile.

Dr. Expert mentions that Kelli's relapsing seemed to begin prior to the stimulants being dispensed by the VA. Well yes, this is true. Stunningly, the VA started prescribing Kelli benzodiazepines again. Specifically Clonazapam, which as listed above, warns of potential side effects, including psychosis.

I vividly remember the meeting with Ms. --- and it was by my request, not Ms. ---'s, that we meet with Kelli together. I was always trying to desperately try to help Kelli and stop her from taking the meds that the VA was supplying her. Kelli came into the meeting completely willingly and unknowingly that I would be there. I said something that made her upset and she left.

After reading this chart though, I regret that day deeply. What had transpired over the years was criminal as far as I'm concerned and I should have not ambushed my sister, but instead, ambushed the chief of staff again with questions, just as I did years earlier.

Dr. Expert suggests that its "unclear" as to whether Kelli was taking any stimulant medications at the time of her admission to VBPC, while it was "clear" that she was using marijuana at that time. Her urine was negative for amphetamines and positive for cannabis. However, according to my "internet" research, amphetamines only show up in urine 1-3 days out while marijuana shows up to a month out. So she could have smoked a joint 29 days earlier for all he knew. What was clear is that her stimulant use was recent. He also states that Kelli had stopped taking all of her medications. However, that's an incorrect statement. On page 1 of the discharge summary, Kelli stated that "she has not been taking her medications as prescribed." It says nothing about stopping her meds.

Dr. Expert suggests that Kelli stopping her Seroquel over a month prior to admission was likely a cause for her psychotic relapse. I think this is highly unlikely. First of all, Kelli would never stop taking her Seroquel because she relied on it to sleep. Secondly, when Kelli would become paranoid, psychotic etc…she usually didn't know what day it was let alone which meds she stopped taking and when. On this admission, Kelli was taping vents in her condo to prevent things from coming through them. She was having paranoid delusions, so how one could suggest confidently that Kelli knew which meds she was taking is questionable Doctor.

Dr. Expert mentions in this section the incident regarding our trip to Pittsburgh during Easter. I know without question that Kelli was taking Seroquel because both my mom and I asked her to stop. She insisted that she could not sleep without it.

Kelli in short became extremely paranoid and believed that Denise was trying to hurt my son Brady. Kelli attacked her on Easter morning. Kelli actually had a screwdriver in her pocket as a weapon. Kelli was admitted to Jefferson Regional Medical Center.

(Pages 855-859) Kelli sees Dr. --- again on 5/29/09. She informs him of her 2 psychiatric admissions since seeing him last. Somehow he concludes that she is "doing much better overall" **He continues her on her current regimen. This is where he notes in caps… "DO NOT RETURN TO STIMULANT MEDICATIONS!"**

He also notes… "discussed need to be tapered off Klonopin Clonazapam) over next 6 months (has signif hx of benzo dependence).

Knowing this, I'm curious as to why she was

continued on this drug to begin with. Also, Klonopin (Clonazapam) is not meant to be used long-term to begin with.

Kelli was prescribed Klonopin through 6/23/10, only months before she died. Also, she was prescribed stimulants through 12/4/09.

(Pages 834-837) Kelli sees Dr---, a new resident that's assigned to Kelli. Kelli informs Dr. --- "I have been seeing Dr. ---, a psychiatrist in the community cause it's hard to have doctors change often". Obviously, she's very forthcoming in telling Dr. --- this in my opinion. Kelli informs Dr. --- that Dr. --- has been prescribing her Aplenzin and regular Adderall for ADD. Again, this was extremely forthcoming and transparent on Kelli's part in my opinion.

(Page 836) Dr. --- orders a 60 day supply of Adderall. Surprisingly, she notes on the same page, "Although Dr. ---'s assessment, it was interfering with her mood swings."

So regardless of the fact that he/she knew Kelli apparently was receiving Adderall from an outside physician; Dr. --- blatantly ignores Dr. ---'s note to stop stimulants. And knowing Kelli's long history of prescription drug history, Dr. --- still prescribes Adderall and Klonopin.

Kelli was admitted into VBPC again on 1/8/10. On 1/6/10, the VA dispensed #60 Clonazapam.

According to VBPC records, Kelli was admitted voluntarily due to abusing her Klonopin, Adderall and Fioricet. She was suffering from decreased self-care, related to substance abuse and depressive symptoms. Kelli's chief complaint was "I'm so agitated, lifeless, I'm basically hooked on pills. My health and my mind is shot."

Dr. Expert suggests that Kelli was "minimizing" her substance abuse history all along to the treating doctors at the VAMC while obtaining different medications either from other community providers or by purchasing them on the street. However, I think this statement is ridiculous. Kelli told the VA about Dr. ---, they knew his name and apparently what he was prescribing. Kelli also informed them she was seeing Dr. --- and Dr. --- at one point. She informed them of all of her admissions. It's in my opinion that Kelli was more than forthcoming in her information. **As evident by the Rx Profile package, no one can argue against the fact that the VA prescribed incredibly shocking amounts of dangerous drugs over the years. And there's absolutely no evidence that Kelli ever purchased "street" drugs. She didn't have too according to the Rx Profile. The VA continued to readily supply her drugs, so truly she had no need to venture out onto the street.**

Dr. Expert does not include in his note here that on the day Kelli got discharged from VBPC, 1/14/10, (Pages 827-829), Kelli calls requesting a medication refill. Kelli informs the VA that she had just gotten released from VBPC and that our grandma died, therefore, Kelli has to travel to Pennsylvania for the funeral.

Also, for some reason, this note describes Kelli as "cooperative with good eye contact," even though this is a phone consult.

Kelli was dispensed #540 Seroquel on this very stressful day. She had just got discharged for severe depression in addition to finding out that her grandma died. I can't come up with any good reason why it's necessary to dispense #540 pills of anything? Also interestingly, on the Rx Profile, the quantity is listed as #4, but again, it's supposed to be #540. This specific bottle was found at Kelli's condo and is included in the Medical Examiner's list of meds found. They also gave her #16 Tramadol, although I doubt that the quantity is correct. Very rarely did they ever prescribe something to her in small quantities.

Also, the dangerous and addicting drug Phenobarbital is again dispensed. #120 of these pills were given to Kelli as well on the same day.

I've also come across another incorrect quantity amount on page 8 of the Rx Profile. Valium is listed with the quantity of #1 however; you'll see on page 1286 of Kelli's chart, the quantities should be #120 and #90, not #1.

Dr. Expert speaks here of Kelli's voluntary admission into the VA's outpatient substance abuse program, 1/29/10-2/22/10. Dr. Expert notes that Kelli demonstrated good motivation without paranoia or psychosis. **What Dr. Expert doesn't mention is Kelli's complaint on 2/3/10, (Pages 813-815) "Feel like I'm having withdrawals". I then noticed that on that very day, 2/3/10, the VA dispensed #60 Clonazapam, the same benzodiazepine that she's struggled with for years.**

(Pages 797-800) Kelli sees Dr. --- for the first time on 2/8/10. He states in the eval that she's off of Clonazapam which is simply untrue. In fact, Kelli gets Clonazapam refills on 2/3/10, 6/22/10 and 6/23/10 as identified on page 10 of the Rx Profile. Kelli felt that she suffered from mood swings, which as I listed earlier, can be caused directly from the Clonazapam. They also keep her on Neurontin, an anti-convulsant, which has its own long list of possible dangerous side-effect, including psychosis, depression and anxiety. (page 10 of Rx Profile) He described her mood as "depressed and anxious."

Dr. Expert "suggests" that Kelli becomes psychotic again because she relapsed and started smoking marijuana again. Again, this angers me greatly. On page 68, 2/16/10, Kelli's cannabis result was negative. On page 69, 2/12/10, her test was negative for cannabis.

What was in fact happening is that Kelli was again addicted to Clonazapam and starting to have side effects, ailments etc... some of them the very same as the earlier years of abusing it.

(Pages 744-748)This is where Dr. Expert notes Kelli's overdose of Seroquel on 3/12/10 while at the VA, waiting for transport to Salem. He notes that Kelli admitted to me that she ingested an entire bottle of Seroquel prior to me bringing her to the hospital. I strongly disagree with this. Frankly, this is a complete lie! Kelli took the pills when I went out to my car. (Page 669) She had the pills in her bag of belongings. Kelli was interviewed by both a nurse and doctor prior to this, they knew she was actively suicidal, yet still, neither of them asked her what she had with her as far as meds. Instead, they sent us out to the waiting room, never once asking to go through Kelli's bag. If we weren't at the hospital, Kelli would have died after this overdose. She spent nearly a week in the intensive care unit.

It's also important to note here that Kelli is still actively on Clonazapam, Topamax, Seroquel, and Fioricet.

Kelli's admitted to the ICU on 3/12/10. Dr. Expert states that Kelli had one grand mal seizure, but he failed to mention that in addition to the grand mal seizure, Kelli also had several others as documented in the chart and witnessed by me. (Page 692) She also had moments of decreased oxygen saturations with rhonchus (Page 692). I think it's important not to minimize the danger that Kelli faced after this overdose. (Page 610) On 3/15/10, Hypoxia is noted and Kelli's oxygen is now increased. (Page 546) Kelli's now hypotensive and hypokalemic and cannot transfer out of the ICU. (681) "No lower plan to transfer to a lower level of care."

(668) "PT's sister Darla shows concern about the Datrolene meds since pts eyes are opening to voice in a halfway manner."

(673) 3/13/13 "Pt makes gurgling noises from mouth. Pt had episodes seizures lasted about 30 sec."

I also want to note that Kelli's cannabis test was negative on 3/12/10. (Page 67)

Not surprisingly, even after I asked the physician not to restart the Seroquel when Kelli woke up, it was re-started anyway, in addition the Clonazapam.

(644) "Sister at bedside."

(642) "She was brought in by her sister. Pt's sister reported pt took her entire bottle of Seroquel while she went out to the car for approximately ten minutes."

(638) "Pt. has continued to be very restless

throughout this shift. Talking to unseen persons, picking at the air and attempting to get OOB. Pt. gets very agitated and resistive when attempts at giving comfort care made."

"Pt is more on aggressive behavior, on one occasion pt starts crying." Restraints applied.

(632) "No female bed is available. Attempting to place at Salem."

(618) "Sister at bedside. Given sips of water and juice."

(615) "Called sister and gave her finding of cxr and our concern about aspiration pneumonia and small concern for pulmonary edema."

(614) 3/15/10 "**Patient had decreased breath sounds in the left lung. Cxr is done and shows bilateral air space disease L>R. Reviewed toxicology of Seroquel. Seizure could be from Seroquel also."** (duh!)

(613) 3/15/10 **"Likely suicide attempt with Seroquel with h/o severe depression and recent suicidal ideation per sister."**

"No significant alcohol by history."

"Next of kin is sister: Darla."

(612) 3/15/10 "Admitted with suspected overdose on Seroquel as per sister who is closely involved with patient care."

"Sister reports no h/o significant alcohol use. Patient who is much more alert and oriented this morning when seen reports she drinks once a month and does not over do it."

Dr. Expert states that Kelli eventually admitted to discontinuing her Seroquel and Celexa. I'm not sure however, especially after I showed them pictures of how Kelli was living, that anyone could think in any way, shape or form that she knew what she was or was not taking. **She thought that her water was poisoned and Jesus was talking to her while still attempting to escape the CIA. So I doubt very much that she knew what her meds were. I know according to her records though, she was still receiving Clonazapam,**

Seroquel, Topamax, Clonazapam and Fioricet from the VA.

(Page 662) Not surprisingly, there are no female beds available at the Hampton VA. So now they're trying to send her back to Salem, VA which was devastating to both of us. (Page 451) "Became anxious when told she was to be transferred to Richmond."

Kelli was eventually transferred to VBPC on 3/19/10, but was then forced to transfer back to the VA in just 4 days on 3/23/10 because they had a bed open up. (Page 422) Chief complaint "I don't know why I couldn't stay there." I remember this day vividly like so many others. Kelli called me from VBPC crying hysterically because once again, she's being bounced around.

-End of Review (unfinished…see why in the next chapter)

38
DRIVEN TO MADNESS

Throughout the hearings Bob suggested that if the VA offered a specific settlement amount, that we accept it. Truthfully, we didn't anticipate that they would, but eventually they did. I didn't want to settle. I was still trying to finish the review. I wanted to defend the Kelli I once knew in court. And Bob had a really hard time consoling me after we agreed to settle. I completely fell apart in the judge's chambers. I was an emotional train-wreck, not being able to speak through the tears.

After the agreement in the privacy of the judge's chambers, the official settlement hearing took place in an ostentatious courtroom. I have never before been in a legal bind that would take me to this space. I felt like sixteen years of fear, angst, frustration, and anger were outwardly painted on my face, body, and soul. I was naked and afraid. Afraid that the truth would ultimately be buried in a vault of manila folders. Leaning into the stark ominous microphone I heard the words uttered from my mouth, as if they were not my own, "Yes sir," as I consented to the terms. Then, as my insides suddenly turned to mush revealing a fully compromised sunken chest, I desperately wanted to sternly retract, "Wait, I changed my mind." *I really wanted to. For you Kel. For all that we have shared and would have known always and forever. I'm so sorry. Please forgive me.*

I came home from the settlement hearing, shut my bedroom door, and sobbed myself to sleep. On that day, exactly one month to the day before our scheduled trial date, I felt as though I failed my sister. I couldn't believe that it was ending this way, without the VA having to answer for the reckless medicating, misdiagnosing, and what I saw as unethical medical practices in Kelli's care. The government settled, an exchange for no admission of guilt or any wrongdoing. My only saving grace was thinking future media interviews would have to address this convoluted debacle. The future is now, here, in this memoir. *I won't let you down Kelli.*

I had worked on that review tirelessly and felt strongly that it would eventually become our smoking gun at the trial. It was neither grammatically pretty nor politically correct. But it was accurate, honest, and detailed. It mapped out the years of drugging and I couldn't imagine anyone debating that. Numbers do not lie after all. Speaking of numbers, the settlement was for six figures and I received $12,935.02; with the funeral costs (~$8000) and the balance on Kelli's truck (~$7,000), I paid the difference out-of-pocket. The case became extremely expensive due to expert witnesses, attorney fees, etc. But it was never about money for me. It was about saving Kelli. It was about stopping Kelli from being driven to madness through the endless prescriptions. And now it's about saving the lives of others.

Kelli's overdose on Seroquel in March, the one that landed her in the ICU, was the first of several attempts to end her life with Seroquel. If only the VA had stopped the Seroquel. But they chose not to and Kelli's dead. Kelli overdosed on that specific drug four times during the last year of her life, the fourth killing her. She was dispensed #150 pills in less than one month prior to her death. Within 25 days to be exact. If you read the package insert to Seroquel, it clearly states that if a patient is displaying any signs of suicidal behaviors then you consider stopping the drug. The VA chose not to. Yes, this stuff really happens. Yes, not just to us.

"The military's spending on Seroquel increased sevenfold since 2001 as veterans' doctors prescribed it for insomnia and post-traumatic stress disorder."

(source: http://www.cbsnews.com/news/how-seroquel-a-risky-antipsychotic-became-a-general-purpose-mental-health-drug/)

Kelli's prescriptions started in 2002. Here is more from the same article;

"Injuries from Seroquel's side effects can be severe and permanent. In addition to diabetes they include suicidal/self-injurious behavior, and neurological movement disorders such as tardive dyskinesia, dystonia and parkinsonism. AstraZeneca's role in promoting Seroquel for off-label uses is well documented. The company has paid $1.5 billion in legal costs and settlements for its mismarketing of the drug ($520 million to the Department of Justice; another $743 million in legal costs in unresolved cases through March 2011; and $198 million in civil settlements)."

According to the autopsy report, Kelli died from an Acute Seroquel Overdose. **And for your information "Dr. Expert," the cannabis result was negative.** No alcohol and no illicit drugs.

39
IN HER WORDS

I came across a journal that Kelli kept, beginning on January 1st, 2010, locked away in a safe at her condo. *"If found upon my death: give to my sister: Darla M. Grese,"* is written on the inside cover.

I've struggled with whether to share some of these entries or not in this memoir. But reading the inside back cover, "*If this can help even one person to never stop trying then my duty here is done,*" cements my instinctual desire to do so. I won't share everything, but some I will. Kelli penned personal messages to people that she loved and cared for. The excerpts are written examples of Kelli's gratitude and compassion, even during her darkest of times. But others are painful reminders of Kelli's struggle and fight to survive.

I call this my personal journal to recovery and regaining my place in the world and doing great things! God-driven of course!! I surrender to him and pray that I have a bigger part to play in this crazy world!!

I always admired Kelli's faith, and still do. I struggle to find mine, especially now that Kelli's gone. She had an amazing trust in God and it's because of these few lines, that I chose the title Sister Surrendered.

Contacted Passages, Malibu, a reputable drug treatment facility. Contacted Oprah 2X via website and email. Contacted Dr. Phil months ago-no response. Love Dr. Phil. Contacted NY Times-add for financial donations. Won't stop until I get the help that I need!! Hopefully death won't come first!! VA Health Care sux!! Shameful.

Kelli desperately wanted to get better and went to great lengths, looking for help. Like most, she couldn't afford a long-term treatment facility, so she began seeking help from people with large platforms, hoping they would help. There's a day that I recall vividly that she and I sat in my living room, scanning the web, and making phone calls. I must have called ten to fifteen facilities' throughout the United States, trying to find a place that would accept payment plans that Kelli could afford.

If I survive this, I'll make it my mission to have the mental health/addiction portion of health care reform a priority on some level! It has to be fixed, people are dying!!

Now, this is my mission Kel, I've got this.

It's in God's hands!! I know that. I surrender. Every day is a fight to stay alive!! Every day!

Kel, your fighting is over, and I hope you're resting peacefully now.

I'm trying…God knows I'm trying!! "Why me" doesn't matter at all! Why the hell not me? Something has to happen and my life's purpose will be revealed. My faith is being tested, but it's not the first time! I'll do this! I have to! If not, I'll die trying!

And she did try. She was one of the strongest individuals I've ever known. People ask me if I'm angry that she took her own life. And my response is immediate "No! Kelli tried as hard as she could to fight her disease, experiencing anguish that's indescribable."

My mind is giving up!! My body hurts and the darkness and hopelessness is setting in at lightning speed! God is near me though! I can feel him! God help me!!

I envied her faith.

Just left my sister's house! God I love that baby!! I've been trying to see my nephew as much as possible so he always remembers me and remembers how much I loved him!!

He knows Kel and I promise, he'll never forget!

God please take over and give me life for a little while longer!! I think my sister knows something's up!! Can see the worry in her eyes!! I'm trying Dar!! I'm, giving it everything I got!! I'm not dead yet! God's next to me!!

We knew each other on a unique level that I tried to convey in this book. She was right. I was worried.

My sister just sent me a pic over my cell phone of the baby sleeping with his blanky that I bought him and he's hooked on it. She knows though!! I knew it-she's keeping me alive by giving me reasons not to give up!! God's using her to help me!! I can't imagine my life without my sister!! I can't explain what it's like to be a twin!! It's like you have one heartbeat!! If hers quit, mine would to!

My heartbeat is definitely different now, at times, fast and irregular. My heart is still repairing itself, although it'll never be whole again. It can't be.

I put my sister thru hell and back! I mean absolute hell and back!! She's had to involuntarily commit her own twin sister multiple times! I'm so sorry Dar!! I hate who I am! I pray to be that person AGAIN one day so you never have to worry about me again!! I hear your prayers for me!! I truly do!! Keep on Keepin on!!

Kel, I loved who you were and I'm so proud of how hard you fought, how deeply you loved, and how loyal you were to the ones' that you loved, especially Brady. There are days now that I pray for just half of the strength that you had. You were a warrior and I'm so proud to call you my twin sister.

If I'm meant to be a statistic, then I'll fight until God takes me himself!! I slept with the bible and a book written by Joel Olsteen every night for the past five days or so!! Can't read them now, but those books make me feel safe!

I hated that you didn't feel safe Kel, but you're safe now.

I've always loved to write, my sister does too. I always thought I would have had at least one book out already and I end up writing to I don't even know who? There's a real good chance I'll get in a mood and destroy it like I've done to so many others.

Kel, I've written the book for you, just as I promised you I'd do. Your words will make a difference, I promise you.

Rescue me from myself!! Then use me to help others in such desperate, hopeless situations.

Your death will not be in vain Kel.

I'm not special, but I am someone who will go to extremes if I believe in something strong enough!! How long do you keep going though?? I'm still breathing so my mission is nowhere near complete!! Livin' on a prayer-that's all we can do anyways!!

You're wrong Kel, you were special and because of your death, your mission continues through me.

My sister's terrified, and I feel it!! Maybe she's having visions of me gone too? I don't know!! She's giving it all she got too! My world is crashing down around me and I don't have that will to live like I did last week! Hard to admit, but true!! I feel nothing actually!!

This is what a person who suffers from depression can feel like, sad, but true.

Truth is, I want God to take me when he's ready, but please hurry if this is my destiny. Can't live like this much longer!

I hope you've found peace Kel, and I have no doubt that you're in heaven, with God. Your heart was golden and your soul pure, and God knew that.

I love you Dar!!! I know how hard you're praying for me to be ok again!! I hear those prayers and see it in your eyes!! Xoxoxo

And I hope you hear my prayers now Kel, I miss you.

I would give anything and everything to just have someone hold me right now and love me thru this, but that didn't happen!! I need rescued at this point. I pray for it.

You were loved by so many and still are. I knew you were lonely, and that tormented me.

This has been a 12/13 year battle. I've reached out over the years, but here I am! I'm empty.

You never stopped fighting Kel. The system failed you.

Talked to Morna (my accountant friend) today! I love her! A true, true friend!

I remember Kelli speaking of her, with only nice

things to say.

Gina texted me today, my "ex-roomie." Blessed to have her in my life again! Gina knows me very well and knows about my past and has never judged me for it!! I miss her and Cabo dog.

Kelli thought very highly of Gina. She was a great friend to Kelli.

Then there's Kelly. Good looking as hell, covered in tattoos, rides a Harley etc. He is truly my best friend!! Make sure if this is found that he knows how much I adored him!! He has seen me at my worst and has never left my side! I pray he finds an amazing woman and lives happily ever after!! She would be the luckiest woman alive. I love you babe.

Well Kel, your wish came true. "Boy Kelli" found an amazing woman and they are living happily ever after. Her name's Robin and I have no doubt that you'd approve!

In a very dark place!! Just think I'm waiting for my heart to stop. Sounds sick, but I think that's what I'm doing. Don't know anymore!!

After watching what you went through for so many years, I understand why you felt this way, I really do.

Can't be committed again!! Will die before that happens!! Handcuffed, strip searched, treated like a criminal or crazy person! Never again!

We need to change this. No more police cars. Transport patients in unmarked vehicles and treat them with dignity, they deserve that.

I love Danielle more than words can say, but she lives in Cali now and I miss her!! She got me a great coaching gig!! Trust her with my life!! I would do anything and everything for her!! Kjersti to! My other sister.

Danielle and Kjersti were like family to Kelli and still are to me. We've known each other for years, stemming back to our Navy days. Kelli loved them both tremendously and so do I.

Mum, don't you dare flip out if you lose me!! I don't think a daughter could possibly love a mother more than Darla and I love you!! Please find happiness somehow mum! You have to live still, Brady and AJ need you! Dar, move her here ASAP!

Kel, mummy and I are trying to help each other.

We're both struggling, but we're trying. Please know that I'm keeping close tabs on her, just as we always have.

This is why I don't own a gun! When your mind goes, it really does go!! You're outside of yourself almost (no sense).

It wasn't your fault. Your mind became a prisoner of the effects of the pills. It wasn't your fault.

God's with me! I feel him so strongly!! Very peaceful feeling right now!! Of course the pills are bringing me way down but I feel no pain at all! Guess that's what numbing yourself is.

If I could do just one thing over again, I would have taken out a loan, and sent you to that facility in Arizona. There, you could have gotten off of the medications, including the Seroquel, and you would have found peace and comfort within yourself. But I didn't, and you're gone. And I hate that. I should have made that call.

Diagnosed with PTSD while still in the service! My sister and I were stationed overseas at the time! Treatment sucks now! Here, take this pill!

This says enough.

System needs changed!! Morally, just wrong!! This is how we treat our Veterans? So let's medicate the hell out of her though!! That's how vets are treated!! Sorry Gov't.

"Go Steelers" LOL Now I'm just writing things that pop into my head! Brady's first pic was taken in a Pitts Steeler's outfit-say no more. My favorite number is #12 for Terry Bradshaw and has been since I was little. America's Team!

I had to address this because of our love of the Steelers. Every year I walk with Team Kelli during the Out of the Darkness Walk. Our shirts are black and gold with a number 12 on the back. Even Rocco has a shirt and walks with us.

Favorite animal-by far the dog!! My love for them is indescribable.

One of Kelli's last Facebook posts was "DOG is GOD spelled backwards for a reason."

I have to mention my Aunt Marie! That's where I get my middle name from!! We call her "dork" just cause she's silly sometimes! She was our second mom growing up!! I love her, Paul, Kelsee and Chanele more than words could ever say!! Please dork-

Brady needs you and mummy!! Promise me Brady will have a family no matter what!! Xoxoxo

Our relationship with Marie (Ree) is special, which is why one of Kelli's last phone calls was made to her. Our bond is not your typical "niece-aunt" bond. It's just different.

I call Denise sis for a reason!! She truly is my sister-in-law! She and her family have been a true family to Brady since day 1.

Kelli adored Denise, they shared a special friendship. They were family.

This is beginning to feel like a living will almost. Plan on getting mortgage protection so no-one gets stuck with my shit!! Plan on doing that tomorrow morning, God willing! Sell my truck. Sell my story. Do whatever you have to do to prevent financial hell from me.

Sorry Kel, kept the truck, can't bring myself to get rid of it. I'm taking great care of it.

To my brother: I only hope you know how much I've loved you!! I love you baby brother.

Kelli always called our brother Andy, "Baby Brother," even though he's bigger than us.

Dad, I'm proud to have many of your qualities. Esp. when things break, I can fix it myself. I learned a lot from you dad, keep on fishing.

Our father always told us to have our own toolbox and to never rely on a man to fix it for us. And now, with my tools and Kelli's, my garage looks like the tools section in Walmart.

Never understood how people could kill themselves, but I get it!!! I truly get it now. Don't Stop Believing"-love that song!!

This is why I chose to have that song played during Kelli's funeral service.

Love boats too! Probably got that from my father! Being or looking out into the open sea is the most peaceful/surreal feeling ever.

I agree, I love the water as well, there's no greater peace.

Loved the military, was born to wear that uniform!! Love this country and would give my own life if need be!

Kelli was one of the most patriotic individuals you

would ever meet. She truly did love this country, which makes her Veteran's Day death symbolic.

Dar - I'm not me anymore-I'm not controlling my choices in a coherent way. Don't' know how to word it. I'm so afraid right now!

I know Kel, it's okay.

I want/need to be in a better place Dar!! Please live your life for "our" beautiful baby boy, "baby dangerous". He needs you... Do not stop living! God will guide you to peace one day! Trust me. And don't worry where I end up-I'll be in HEAVEN.

I hope you're right Kel, and I'm waiting for his guidance.

Do what you want with this Dar!! Keep it, get rid of it, burn it, whatever gives you the most peace!! Maybe a charity can use a typed copy of this journal if it even makes sense?? They can use it as a learning tool!! This maybe was my purpose Dar-to die and die for a bigger purpose!! I will try and write to the very end!! This can maybe give people hope to never stop trying and to never give up.

Kel, I'd never burn your words, after all, that's all I have left that's tangible. I hope you're right, I hope your story inspires people to fight harder, never surrendering to the disease.

So proud of you Dar. All the work has paid off. You were amazing to watch and it's about time you hit the big screen.

Kelli was my biggest fan!

I love you so much Dana!! You've been an amazing, amazing friend. Not just to me but to everyone and anyone around you!! If angels exist on earth!! She's one of them!! By far. Her girlfriend Angie is great to! Angie knows how to have a good time. LOL I have a blast with you buddy!!

Dana is a part of my family now.

When I yell at God, I really don't see him in the room or anything! Just wanted to clear that up, guess I have some sanity left.

This is another great example of how funny Kelli was.

My sister and I are hooked on "Dancing with the Stars!" Completely hooked.

I still love the show but it's not the same without

being able to call Kelli during commercials. She always hoped that one day I'd get on the show so she could come for the taping. One of my fondest memories is when Kelli and I went to one of their shows in Hampton, VA. We screamed like two school girls. It was so much fun! And ironically, Marie Osmond was in the show.

Our health care system is not in any way, shape or form set up to handle so many people dying every single day!! When I'm gone, I truly hope my sister does something with this journal!! Do whatever you have to do to save lives Dar!!

Trying Kel, I am.

Bring me back God-give me my life-keep my mind strong and my body intact!! I love you God, but I need you today! I surrender to you! I love you and I believe in you.

Her faith in God became stronger and stronger, it never wavered, ever.

If I'm on my way out-I'm sure the hell gonna plug her movie!! Why the hell shouldn't I?? She is-truly the owner of half of my entire heart and soul!! Can't explain the whole "twin thing", but man it's nuts. Know this is just the beginning for you Dar!! You deserve and work hard for it and you're freaking great at it!! I could not be more proud of you.

Everyone should have a supporter like I had in Kelli. I was so lucky to have her rooting for me.

I have to give a shout out to Brandy! She's become a great friend and has checked on me every day! Blessed to have such great friends!!

I don't recall ever meeting Brandy, but thank you for caring about my sister.

The End. Peace Out. Xoxoxo.

I'm ready to go to a better place now!! I'm ready-

40
LEARNING TO WALK AGAIN

It's been three years now since Kelli's been gone, but for me three minutes. At times, I feel stuck. And as time has passed, the personal messages and phone calls have lessened, people have moved on and that's understandable. I've had many moments of loneliness, longing for my sister's backing. Unless you're a twin, it's hard to understand what twin-loss is, but trust me when I say, it's debilitating at times. It's like learning to walk again, one step at a time, without your crutch that keeps you from falling. Even local musician Jessica Doran, being a twin herself, was inspired to write a song after hearing about Kelli's story. The fact is, I don't know how to live as an individual and I need some help working through this. I've actually decided to look into a facility, that ironically Kelli and I looked into for her, located in Arizona. According to my therapist, The Meadows' reputation in dealing with trauma goes unmatched. Through the help of intensive weekly counseling, which I highly recommend by the way, I've learned that I too suffer from PTSD, caused by the years leading up to Kelli's death, and her death in and of itself. I need to process her death, something I'm pretty sure I've not done yet. Instead, I've focused my energy on parenting, working, the lawsuit, writing, part-time acting, keeping up the house, and anything else I could distract myself with. And proudly, I've done a decent job with the exception of acting. I haven't landed a significant role since Kelli's death which I attribute to low self confidence and anxiety. Just auditioning for me now, is at times, very uncomfortable. But I'll continue my pursuit in following my dream, regardless.

Brady and I have an amazing relationship. I'm not great at a lot of things, but parenting, I'm great at. As a matter of fact, I'm great at worrying about everything and everyone else except me. After all, I've never had to deal with myself because I've always concentrated on helping everyone else in my life. So taking care of me is a foreign concept. But I have to learn. I just do. So hopefully soon, I'll leave home for a month, maybe longer, and work with professionals who can teach me the tools that I need to continue on twin-less.

This memoir was initially a screenplay which I did in fact complete only months after Kelli's passing. It sits on my nightstand. It wasn't long before Kelli died that she jokingly suggested that I write a screenplay about us and then we would play ourselves. I laughed it off, reminding her that she couldn't act and hated being on camera. But after losing her, I wished I would have responded by saying, "Kel, let's write it together, and once it's finished, we'll figure the rest out."

Although I feel strongly that the VA Hospital was responsible for Kelli's death and years of anguish, I must also say that I feel just as strongly that the VA does in fact have great doctors, who in fact, care about their patients, mine included. I do not believe that any Veteran, ever, should hesitate in going to a Veterans Affairs Hospital because of what I've written. However, I do believe by telling Kelli's story that certain practices the VA Hospitals adhere to will be looked at, hopefully. I believe that when appropriately prescribed, medicines are necessary and they're proven to work. But it's when they're prescribed irresponsibly that they can result in dire consequences, including death and suicide.

I've wrestled the temptations of including excerpts from depositions and medical record reviews. When I first began writing this book I had every intention of including some, knowing they would solidify whatever doubts some might have of my claims of irresponsible practices. But I've decided against that. This memoir has become something so much more than initially intended. It's become a documented journey, while only barely scratching the surface, of two sisters whose love for each other was unprecedented. And surprisingly, it's also become an outlet for me to speak candidly and honestly about my struggles since Kelli's death. And this will shock most that know me, aware of my desire for privacy.

I still remain friends with Mike Strickland, who's now the Lead Funeral Director at Family Choice Funeral and Cremations in Virginia Beach. My gratitude to him truly is endless. It's because of him that I'm left with the vision of Kelli looking peaceful, and that's a gift that continues to give, not only to me, but to my family.

Our loyalty was steadfast and our devotion to one another, solid. Our love was unconditional, no matter what the circumstances, and I'm so grateful every day for the memories of the joy and laughter that we shared together. Intellectually, I know that the bond that Kelli and I shared is impossible for anyone to replace, but I find myself longing for someone to fill at least a small portion of it, which is another reason for my need to seek professional help. One day, Brady will grow up into a healthy man, meet a wife, and start a family of his own. And I find myself now, even with him only six, dreading the day that he'll leave me. And that's a huge burden for a child to carry. I need to find happiness within myself and I'm learning that it's not as easy as I anticipated it to be. When you're a twin, loneliness is somewhat unfamiliar, because you've always had each other. So when a twin passes, the other is left unprepared.

Grieving Kelli's death is a process that I've grown to despise, taking me on an emotional roller coaster that I can't get off of. There are days when I think I'm feeling better, but then, all of a sudden; I feel the need to scream uncontrollably. Or I'll take the opposite alternative and lay in bed for a few hours, feeling sorry for myself. It's amazing how I'm able to trick my brain into justifying that it's okay for me to curl up in a ball, for most of the afternoon, pouting.

These past few years have changed me for sure. My world is completely different. It always will be. And I'm doing my best to learn the ropes of this new life that I'm now faced with. I'm not perfect, and I've struggled. I've lashed out. I'm guarded and the ability to trust anyone with the heart that I have left is minimal. Truth is, I have no reserve left and sometimes that scares me.

As Brady grows older, I can see Kelli's sense of humor in him, plain as day. He's just as witty as she was, and I love that about him, amongst so many other things. He loves playing baseball, and he's great at it. But I have yet to attend a game where I haven't spent at least an inning fighting back the tears, wishing Kelli was standing at first base, coaching his team. And he loves to fish, casting his line just as well as me, if not better. He's my little buddy. And we talk about Kelli often, having more discussions about heaven than I'd like to admit. Like most children, he's very curious, asking countless questions about why his Aunt Kelli died so young. I still struggle to answer that question, each time he asks it.

And we even hatched our own baby duck, naming him Quackers. It was an incredible experience which ended up turning my kitchen into a science lab. Brady's love for animals is identical to mine and I wouldn't have it any other way. And who knows, maybe one day we'll even have a turkey.

I've stressed a little about who I'd mention in this book, nervous that I'd hurt someone's feelings by not mentioning their names. But I've realized that it's impossible to do. Kelli had so many great friends, some I've never even met. I'm blessed as well. I've had so many notes and messages from friends over the past three years. And I've done my best to acknowledge each one of them.

I need each person to know, who's taken the time to reach out to me, in whatever capacity, that if it weren't for your heartfelt show of support and love, I don't know that I'd be able to muster the energy to get out of bed, much less write this book on some days. From the bottom of my heart, "Thank you."

41
KELLI'S PLACE

Sixteen years ago I was ignorant to mental illness and addiction. But witnessing Kelli's torment and struggle to survive opened my eyes to a world that most only read about or watch in movies. I have gained an even greater empathy for anyone who struggles with depression, mental illness, and/or addiction. But still, there's a stigma attached to those words that's unjust and offensive. My twin sister was just one of many patients that some might mock. As compassionate human beings, we must remember, just as cancer and diabetes are both diseases, so are mental illnesses and addiction.

I have dreams of opening up a **LONG-TERM** facility locally **JUST FOR WOMEN** who are fighting depression, addiction, and mental illness. **KELLI'S PLACE**. Kelli was always so uncomfortable, feeling vulnerable, around male patients. Even though I do completely empathize with both men and women with these conditions, I still feel strongly that women need their own facility. I envision cutting a black and gold ribbon and inviting women in for a minimum thirty day stay instead of a three to five day stabilize-and-release practice.

PICTURES AND JOURNAL ENTRIES

Kelli is the pretty one with her hands touching.

Kelli is wearing the solid shirt on our
Eighteenth birthday.

Kelli's fishing at Lake Whitehurst (Norfolk, VA). Her favorite form of relaxation. The beautiful sunset reminds me of her spirit.

Our Color Guard days at Portsmouth Naval Hospital. I'm holding the rifle as Kelli chats with a teammate. We are anxiously awaiting a Veterans Day Ceremony.

Our graduation photo taken at boot camp.
Best day ever!
Kelli is by the flag of course.

One of my favorite photos of Kelli and Brady.
She loved him so much.

This is the last photo of Kelli and Brady together. I cry every time I see it. I don't know what to say.

A small window into the disarray that was expressed through Kelli under the influence of the medications.

The dirty laundry piled up all over Kelli's condo. Looking back, it seems symbolic of being buried by the effects of the prescriptions.

Kelli duct taped every opening in her condo, including air vents. She had hallucinations of toxic substances coming into the living space.

Jesus Loves Mia etched into Kelli's bedroom wall.

I miss you every minute of every day.

PARTIAL MED LIST FOR KELLI

DRUG	CLASS	Page	1998	1999	2000	2001	2002	2003	2004	2005	2006	2007	2008	2009	2010
Phenergan	Antihistamine-sedative	3			160	160								360	120
Atarax	Antihistamine-sedative	3			40	80									
Vistaril	Antihistamine-sedative	3													126
Percocet	Narcotic	6		40	[illegible]	120									
Tylenol with Codeine	Narcotic	6			360	120						240			
Codeine Sulfate	Narcotic	6				30									
Demerol	Narcotic	6	120		240	80									
Fioricet	Barbiturate	7	240	240	1140	420	780	840	420	300	360	480	360	300	60
Phenobarbitol	Barbiturate/sedative	8								84	56				120
Valium (Diazepam)	Benzodiazepine	8			[illegible]	[illegible]	120								
Ativan (Lorazepam)	Benzodiazepine	8	450										60		90
Clonazapam(Klonopin)	Benzodiazepine	9,10	750	[illegible]	[illegible]	720							120	240	240
Buspirone	Sedative/Hypnotic	9	60						360	720		1080	360		
Carbamazepine	Anticonvulsant	9													840
Divalproex	Anticonvulsant	10	60							90					
Gabapentin(Neurontin)	Anticonvulsant	10	240		240										1290
Topamax	Anticonvulsant	10,11								810	810				170
Doxepin	Tricyclic antidepressants	11		630	[illegible]	840									
Amitriptyline	Tricyclic antidepressants	11			330										
Aripiprazole	Antispychotic	13,14										30	45	120	
Seroquel	Antipsychotic	14,15					1080	1980		[illegible]	2700	1545	1860	360	1744
Ziprasidone	Antipsychotic	15								120	180				
Lithium Carbonate	Antimanic									120					
Adderall	Amphetamine	16											120	180	
Dextroamphetamine	Amphetamine	16								60					
Ritalin	Psychostimulant	16											60	120	

This is the spreadsheet that I created to count the medications. I needed to document it regularly to make sure I was seeing the numbers right. There were so many pills, so often. This is only some of the meds dispensed over the years.

DARLA GRESE, Administrator of the Estate of KELLI MARIE GRESE, Deceased,

Plaintiff,

v.

UNITED STATES OF AMERICA,

Defendant.

Reading this still intimidates me, even after settling the case.

Re: Estate of Kelli Grese

Dear Darla:

We are off and running. The United States has answered the lawsuit. As suspected, they denied all of the important parts and they denied any responsibility for your sister's death. That was to be expected. I am now serving written questions on the government and they will soon be serving written questions on us. As soon as I get them, I will forward them to you. The next step is for the court to notify us that we can come down to set a trial date. I expect to get that notification shortly and I would think we will be setting a trial date sometime in late April. As I told you previously, that will give us a trial date in November.

I'll keep you posted. I hope you are doing well.

Very truly yours,

Robert J. Haddad

The actual letter from Attorney Robert Haddad. I am very grateful for his representation.

These are black bracelets with gold letters that I ordered for the Veteran X and Hope graduates. They are the official program bracelet.

Aunt Marie, my mom, and me at the Out of the Darkness Walk at Mt. Trashmore in Virginia Beach. I raise money each year for Team Kelli to help raise suicide awareness.

JAN 2 2010 5:33pm

* just left my sisters House! God I love that baby!! Iv been tryin to see my nephew as much as possibl So he always remembers me + remember how much I Loved Him!!

I want/need to be in a better place DAr!! Please Live your Life for "our" Beautiful Baby boy "Baby Dangerous☺"!! He needs you

*I have 3 nephews!!

Brady
Jeremy
AJ
+
one on the way

God Bless them ALL ☺

I'LL be watching! ♡ Aunt Kelli
No matter what ~
A Love Like no other!!

XOXOXOXO

6:10 pm
* Still can't turn on the Computer! Nerves are shot!!
→ my sister just sent me a pic over my cell phone of the baby sleeping with his blanky that I bought him & hes hooked on it ☺ She knows though!! I knew it – She's keeping me alive by giving me reasons not to give up!! Gods using her to help me!! I can't imagine my life without my sister!!! I can't explain what its like to be a twin!! its like you have "one" heartbeat!! If hers quit, mine would to!!

6:22pm
Iv put my sister thru hell & back! I mean Absolute Hell & back!! She's had to involuntarily committ her own twin sister MULTIPLE times! I'm So Sorry DAR!! I hate who I am!

FYI:
Im currently taking:
And ?? Adderral (lethal)
Some Klonopin (sedative)
Antidepressant?? Fouricet (barbiturate
Seroquel/ for sleep/

Don't know what to do next or
who to contact that I haven't
already tried in one way or
Another!! God → I wanted a
miracle today!! Don't we all though!!
Im not special, but I am
Someone who will go to extremes
if I believe in something strong
enough!! How long do you keep
going though?? Guess until your
physically or mentally incapable!!
Im still breathing so my mission
is no where near complete!!
Livin on a prayer = thats all we
can do anyways!!!

my sisters terrified + I feel it!!
maybe she's having visions of me gone
to?? I don't know!! She's giving
it all she got to! they all are!
my world is crashing down around
me + I don't have that will to
live that I had just last week!
hate to admit, but true!! I feel
nothing actually!! mindless!! I
hope whatever happens happens like
Tomorrow!! Treatment/Death =
whatever I was meant to
choose between! the courage
to go on or let your mind
and body just go!! It really
is possible to control at least
some of your destiny!!
I chose TX but thats lookin
like just another empty dream!
Truth is = I want God to take me
when hes ready but please hurry if
this is my destiny! Can't live
like this much and/or any longer!

I love you DAR!!! I know how hard
your praying for me
to be OK again!!
I hear them prayers, &
see it in your eyes!!
XOXOXO

* I feel like this "Journal" to
Recovery is more like a living
will, except I have nothing
to leave behind! Just my words!!

them for you!! Do what you want with this Dar!! [illegible]

Keep it, get rid of it, burn it, whatever gives you the most Peace!! maybe a charity can use a "typed" copy of the journal if it's even makes sense?? They can use it as a learning [illegible] tool!! whatever you desire & no guilt!! no guilt ever for any of this! This maybe was my purpose Dar. – To die & die for a bigger purpose!! I will try to write up until the very end!! this can maybe give people hope to never Stop trying & never give up & I don't know anymore!

Klon. Kicken In big time

The End JAN 7, 2010 4:46pm

Peace out :)

XOXOXO

I'm Ready to go to a better place now!! I'm Ready

I call this my personal journey to Recovery & regaining my place in the world + doing great things! God-driven of course!! I Surrender to him + pray that I have a bigger ~~part~~ part to play in this crazy world!!

Always + Forever
Your twin, Kelli

ABOUT THE AUTHOR

Darla M. Grese is a twin sister who lost her better half to side effects from prescribed medications. As a U.S. Navy Veteran, she is an advocate of Veteran X and Veteran Hope programs that address mental illness, PTSD, and unintentional addiction issues. Both programs are sponsored by the Veteran Affairs Medical Center and focus on Veteran recovery and independence. She raises money for Team Kelli and annually participates in the Out of the Darkness Walk at Mt. Trashmore in Virginia Beach (http://www.sos-walk.org/sos/). While continuing to bring awareness to this cause, being a loving parent is her favorite passion and the main focus of her life. Darla's love for the arts has been expressed as a talented actress with appearances in *The F.B.I. files*, *The New Detectives*, *Diagnosis Unknown*, *Wicked Attraction*, Discovery Channel's *The Haunting*, and the movie *Atlantis Down*. She currently works full time as a respiratory therapist at a trauma center in Norfolk, Virginia.

Made in the USA
Lexington, KY
03 February 2018